THE AGE
OF STEAM

H. REID

THE AGE OF STEAM

A Classic Album of American Railroading

by

Lucius Beebe
& Charles Clegg

PROMONTORY
PRESS
New York

ACKNOWLEDGMENTS

For their many kind offices and good gifts of pictures, either of their own photography or artistry or from collections of which they are owners or custodians, the authors are in the debt of the following: Miss Ina Aulls of the Denver Public Library, William Barham, Truman Blasingame, Lee Beaujon, Kent W. Cochrane, Hugh M. Comer, Gordon S. Crowell, Ivan Dmitri, Jim Ehernberger, Howard Fogg, J. B. Fravert, Paul Frenzeny, Charles Grahame, Henry R. Griffiths, Jr., E. S. Hammack, Dr. Philip Hastings, Robert Hale, Harpel's of Lebanon, Doyle B. Inman, George Inness, Fred Jukes, Al Kalmbach and David Morgan of *Trains*, Franklin A. King, Richard Kindig, Paul E. Larson, Robert Le Massena, the Estate of Reginald Marsh, A. C. McClure, William D. Middleton, Beaumont Newhall of George Eastman House, Joseph Pennell and the National Gallery at Washington, H. W. Pontin, H. Reid, William Rittase, Dan Sanborn, Richard Steinheimer, Jim Shaughnessy, David Strassman, Jules Tavernier, Walter Thrall, Jr., Leslie V. Suprey, Joe R. Thompson, A. R. Waud, C. W. Witbeck, and A. P. Withall. They are also grateful to the publicity and advertising departments of many railroads, to Culver Service, Railroad Photographs and to other public sources and depositories of pictorial material of all sorts. Should any names be here omitted it is hoped that credit lines in their appropriate place may in part rectify this deficiency.

The title-page photograph shows action on the Denver & Rio Grande Railroad narrow gage on Cumbres Hill out of Chama with an old Grant engine ahead and two Baldwin diamond stacks behind in the year 1907. From the collection of Fred Jukes.

Published in 1994 by

Promontory Press
A division of Budget Book Service, Inc.
386 Park Avenue South
New York, NY 10016

Promontory Press is a registered trademark of Budget Book Service, Inc.

Library of Congress Catalog Card Number: 72-86410
ISBN: 0-88394-079-5

Printed in the United States of America

"*Somewhere deep buried in the consciousness of every American there lies the image of a steam locomotive*"

CHARLES CLEGG

TABLE OF CONTENTS

FOREWORD

WHEN, in the most moving of American epics "John Brown's Body," Stephen Benét wrote thunderingly of "riders shaking the heart with the hooves that will not cease," he was writing of the centaur chieftains of the Civil War. They were Sheridan, Stuart, Custer, Wheeler, Buford, Forrest, Kilpatrick, Hampton and Lee, the goodliest company of riders to shake the heart in all the history of men on horseback.

But Benét might well have been alluding to another company of riders who, for a century and a half, shook the hearts of the American people as no human artifact or devising has moved or ever will move the spirits and imaginations of men. Not a single generation, but five of them, as men reckon their coming and going on earth, were lifted up by the steam locomotive engine, by its sights and sounds and even its smells which laid so compulsive a hold on the national imagining that it will never entirely disappear from the national consciousness.

The railroad locomotive was incomparably more an instrument of destiny than any other to which the hands of men were turned, even including the Colt's Patent Revolving Pistol. For fifteen decades "the tall, far-trafficking shapes" of American record were the smoke plumes of burning wood, coal and oil that moved with compulsive majesty across the summer horizons of a nation bound on mighty landfarings. They were the tangible symbols and oriflamme of a universal preoccupation with movement and the realization of a continental dimension.

No single aspect of the grand design of American life but had its intimations of railroading.

The War Between the States was, in its final resolution, a war of railroads. One has but to take up any volume of "The Pictorial History of the Civil War" to see where aggression and defense and, most of all, the then unformalized science of logistics followed the panting engines. In the background and often enough in the foreground of an unbelievable number of battles and bivouacs, troop movements and beleaguered cities the light iron rail shows laid on the unsophisticated roadbed of the age.

The westward sweep of people achieved the great third movement of the symphony of Manifest Destiny aboard the cars. When the plains and mountains, the high passes and the singing trestles from Bangor to the Rio Grande were finally laid in a spider's web of transport that joined and converged and terminated with geometric symmetry, a wealthy way of life unknown to any previous generation of men came into being on the hypothesis of the powered wheel riding the bonded rail.

Nor was the symphony of steam entirely scored to a theme of grandeur. There were interludes of less august traffickings where little railroads and obscure branches coiled strongly about the hearts of bread-and-cheese people in far places. The way freight, the twice weekly mixed train, the short-line passenger run, along curving riverbanks and through shady woodlands, all blended the music of their friendly bells with the grand motif of thunderous main lines with presidents in flowered waistcoats and corporate names ending in the magic word "Pacific."

The short line seemed for many years to the authors of this anthology to be possessed of enchantments sometimes absent in main lines with four pairs of track reaching to the farthest horizon and centralized traffic control. Its country ways and homely traffickings over roadbeds which in many cases were already returning to the elemental earth, its hand-me-down motive power maintained from spare parts, lathe-turned before Dewey took Manila, its wayward journeyings across meadows and through woodlands which Thoreau would have admired, seemed to them to provide tangible continuity with the nation's simpler yesterdays and less complicated commitments.

But now the short lines and the main lines of mighty landfarings are all one in the common calamity that has overwhelmed them with the advent of a scheme of things that will lay no hold on the imaginings of generations to come. The princely Union Pacific and the humble Yorktown, Hoopole & Tampico alike bowed to a blighted artifact and the demeaning expediency of a mildewed time.

Only in pictured form will the New York Central's splendid Niagaras and the kingly K-4s of the Pennsylvania grow large as they approach the beholder under far-flung canopies of smoke; only in remembrance will there dwell the sights, sounds and the very smells of railroading in the grand manner.

It is for this melancholy and yet compelling reason that we have compiled this volume of the best pictorial record of American railroading in the century and a quarter of operations that can be called the "age of steam."

In assembling an anthology of the pictorial record of steam in America, the authors have been the objects of such knightly generosity from collectors, photographers and artists in the field that to select any for their special gratitude would be at once invidious and unbecoming. The credit that we are able to give in its conventional place in this book is at best an honorarium, not a reward for rich gifts nobly offered.

If some of our own and, occasionally, other photographs have previously appeared in the editorial economy of our other books on the same subject, we have included them here, too, because these books are out of print and unavailable or because, in all modesty, we consider them classics and necessary of inclusion in a classic portrait gallery.

Virginia City
1957

Lucius Beebe
Charles Clegg

HOWARD FOGG

To the philosopher, John Ruskin, the most deplorable manifestation of the itself deplorable nineteenth century in which he lived was the steam locomotive engine whose tall, crenelated smokestacks and clattering train brigades, filled with people who had no occasion to travel anyway, were destroying the tranquillity of the English countryside. Why, argued the esthete Ruskin, just because a device was useful need it also be hideous? If English railway engines could be designed to resemble the monsters of mythology—say dragons snorting fire from distended nostrils, their functional being clothed in fancy— perhaps they could be excused on the grounds of social expediency. The locomotive (ABOVE), painted by Howard Fogg, was the *Lightning*, outshopped in 1848 by the American Locomotive Works at Schenectady for the Utica & Schenectady Railway. Its chimney would have offended Ruskin, but it was a marvel of efficiency for its time, and in a little while American builders would turn their attention to ornamentation of their product so that, for a time and like the clipper ship, the railroad locomotive would be at once one of the most beautiful as well as useful of all human artifacts.

Rugged individualism was the dominant characteristic of every aspect of early railroading in the United States. Each of the great erecting shops, Hinckley & Drury, Breese Kneeland, William Mason, Amoskeage, Richard Norris & Son, Matthias Baldwin, the Lawrence Machine Shop, Ross Winans, the Portland Company, Taunton Locomotive Works—and there were many others—had their own idea of wheel arrangement, valve gear and boiler design. Hundreds of homemade engines turned out by Yankee blacksmiths and York State mechanics reflected the eccentric genius of a various and self-reliant generation. Rugged individualism also characterized the board rooms and directors' meetings of the first incorporated carriers as is suggested by this scene of internecine strife (BELOW). This was not, as might at first sight be imagined, a war between labor and capital, but a purely internal contest between two factions of stockholders for control of the Albany & Susquehanna Railroad near Harpersville, New York. It was but one of many such stirring encounters in the pre-Cambrian age of railroading. The pose of an ancestral fireboy (LEFT) on the running board of the *Hoosac* suggests the origin of his name "tallowpot," since one of his duties was to grease the valve motion with mutton tallow while the train was moving.

That locomotives of monstrous dimensions and fearsome outline appeared both early and late in the age of steam is suggested on the page opposite by the pictures, comparatively arranged, of a Camden & Amboy large-drivered Crampton locomotive, outshopped in 1849, and one of the Southern Pacific's gargantuan freight-haul Mallets photographed on the run out of Tucumcari, New Mexico, exactly a century later. The similarity ends, however, with the dimension of terror and profile of fearsomeness, for the Southern Pacific's heavy-duty engines were vastly successful, ending out their years of usefulness on the Modoc Division in Nevada, while the Crampton type, ordered by Robert Stevens, president of the Camden & Amboy, and built by Isaac Dripps to English specification, had insufficient adhesion and were soon scrapped. A characteristic of the Camden's motive power was the retention, in the British manner, of a diminutive hutch on the tender top to house a postillion who faced forward into the wind and cinders. A later generation of designers reversed the tender cab so that the head brakeman could survey his train in comparative comfort. One advantage was on every hand admitted for the single-drive-wheel engines: once started they could go as fast as anyone wanted to ride them. Nothing was done to abate the reputation of the locomotive engines of the 'forties by an artist's drawing (ABOVE) of a "Monster Coming Along the Susquehannah Station" precariously on the primitive iron rails laid on stone sleepers, shown below.

In the '40s, Passengers were Seldom Merely Maimed

In the wrecks of the 'forties and 'fifties, as speed gradually increased with few accompanying improvements in car construction or safety generally, few passengers emerged from collisions or derailments merely maimed. The cornfield meet, here depicted, on the Northern Pennsylvania Railroad at Camp Hill Station, fourteen miles from Philadelphia, in 1856, resulted in the death of seventy persons, most of them children, aboard a train chartered by St. Michael's Catholic Church, Kensington. The cars promptly took fire and the scene, "drawn on the spot by our own artist," shortly afterward appeared in *Frank Leslie's Illustrated Newspaper*. In the bottom sketch the train crew and neighbors recovered the maimed and dying from the ruins.

Patrons of the steamcars in New England could occasionally expect catastrophe through the Yankee agency of falling through a covered bridge, as witness this deplorable occurrence on the Vermont & Massachusetts Railroad, now part of the Boston & Maine, near Brattleboro, Vermont, in 1866.

Less lethal than the contingencies portrayed elsewhere on these pages, the hotbox was a minor inconvenience and source of perennial contemporary humor, as portrayed for *Harper's Weekly* by Thomas Worth, a popular sketch artist of the 'seventies.

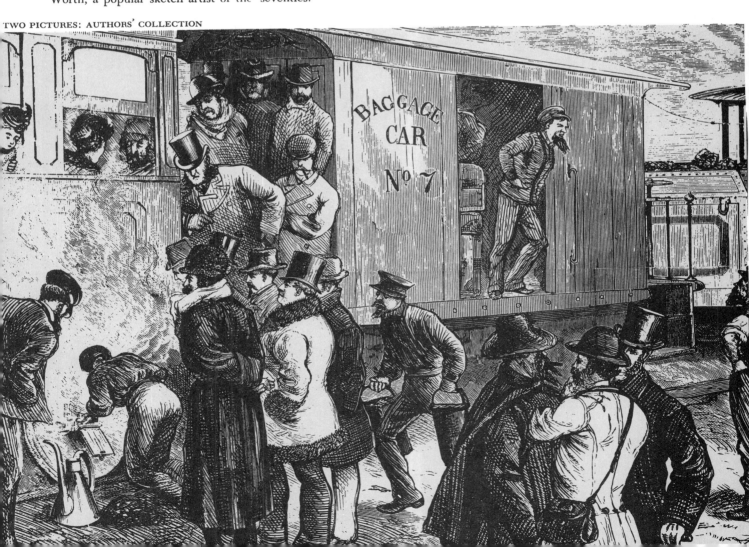

Did the whiskered tallowpot of the Early Ordovician age of railroading, conning the uncertain rails through summer woodlands for bears or the barricades of hostile farmers, foresee the spacious destinies which in a few decades were to spread before his pilot beam in limitless vistas of continental conquest? Perhaps not. More likely he saw only the possibilities of snakeheads in the strap-iron rail beneath his ponderous cowcatcher or of a cornfield meet with the down train around the next curve. But the thing was there, and in. counting houses in Boston and Philadelphia there were men in stock collars with gold-headed walking sticks who saw it as clear as a green light on a long tangent, giving them a clear track to the great American adventure, the ineffable Western land. The men in the stock collars had the key to the safe, and in only a few years the grading gangs were where only Army Engineers and Mountain Men had been before, over the Natchez Trace, across the Great Plains toward Fort Laramie and along the route of bearded old Ben Holladay's Great Central Overland, California & Pike's Peak Express. In time the illimitable iron would come to the greatest trace of all, the Santa Fe Trail, stretching into Spanish yesterdays of overland commerce in gold and Taos lightning. The men in the velvet-collared frock coats saw all these things as they gathered over a glass of Medford rum at Parker's in School Street, and they confided their seeing to William Mason of Taunton and Matthias Baldwin and William Norris of Philadelphia, and the thing was as good as done. Soon weeds would grow on berm and towpath of Clinton's Ditch, the Work of the Age. Ancient clerks would close forever the daybooks of Abbot Downing & Co., in Concord, in the New Hampshire Grants. But along the riverways of York State and in the Everglades and in the high passes of the incredible Sierra the crossheads would flash obedient to the greatest rhythm of all in the symphony of steam.

PHILIP R. HASTINGS

Wherever yard workers and switchmen could raise a thirst, there was a beer saloon handy to the tracks, and the foreman himself would usually lead the parade to the bar at appropriate intervals throughout the working day. It made life easier all 'round. This shady retreat advertised Buffalo Beer for a nickel, evidence of its time and location in the West. It flourished next the Central Pacific tracks in the Sacramento 'eighties. Its counterpart could be found in Kansas City and New Orleans, Tacoma, White River Junction, Albany and Atlanta—a refuge and retreat for strong men of a masculine calling.

The legend, assiduously cultivated in later generations, to the effect that railroad men, from president to callboy, were invariably pillars of the local temperance society has no foundation in fact. A multiplicity of gorgeous saloons, from Bangor to Laredo and from Baltimore to the Golden Gate, were named for the calling of their best customers: the Switch Key, the Time Card, the Crown Sheet, the Order Board, the Whistle Stop, the Semaphore, the Conductor's Rest, the Green Light, the Rear Shack, the Clear Track and the Roundhouse. Railroaders ranked as strong men with the bottle along with cowpokes, lumberjacks, stage drivers, cavalrymen and Mississippi River gamblers. In the nineteenth century, engineers, firemen, conductors and brakemen were, as a rule, younger than they were later to become as an occupation group, and were more durable against proof spirits in the saloons that were handy to every freight yard and terminal in the land. The same was true of upper-echelon railroaders. Division superintendents and general managers, moving in more exalted circles, knew the accepted brands of champagne and smoked imported Havana fancy tales instead of the twofers of the car tonks. Until the coming of Rule G and a correspondingly degenerate age, a high-wheel engineer could be identified by his aroma of bourbon as readily as a drummer by his sample case.

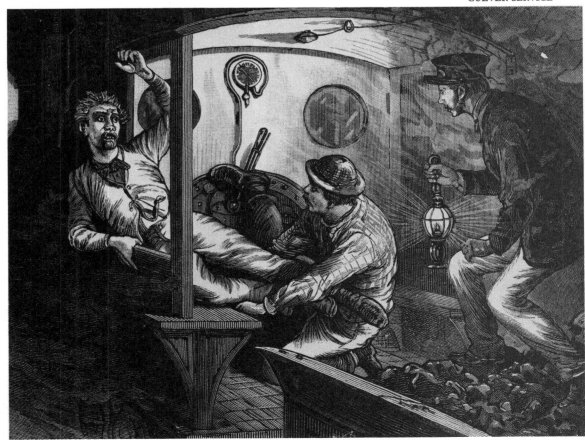

Few engineers of a more robust age carried things as far as Broad Gauge Bosworth of the Erie who had an attack of the snakes near Elmira, New York, in the 'seventies, and had to be restrained by fellow members of the train crew from tossing himself out the cab window.

Classic train wreck of its time was the fearful holocaust at Ashtabula, Ohio, when, in 1876, the Lake Shore & Michigan Southern's crack *Pacific Express* fell through a Howe Truss Bridge (RIGHT) and burned on the frozen surface of a creek 150 feet beneath. The ten baggage, express cars, coaches and Pullmans carried a total of eighty-eight passengers to their deaths. The next day, Charles Collins, chief engineer of the railroad, who had certified the bridge as safe, blew his brains out. Five years later, Amasa Stone, the Lake Shore's president, took his own life, haunted by responsibility for the disaster. The Ashtabula horror was also felt to have contributed to the death, only a few days later, of the aging Commodore Vanderbilt, since the Lake Shore was one of the proudest of the Vanderbilt subsidiaries. Less terrible, since no one was injured, was the stalling in a monster snowdrift at Fairport, New York, the following year, of the New York Central & Hudson River Railroad's *Atlantic Express* (ABOVE). Rescue engines from Palmyra also became derailed until, in all, nine locomotives were snowed into the grandfather of all traffic snarls. Passengers at length had to be rescued in sleighs and the Rochester-Syracuse main line of the railroad was inoperable for more than a week.

Although sleeping cars of various patent designs had been in service for nearly two decades and refreshment cars, notably clubs cars with bar service, were coming into vogue during the Civil War, the first intimations of true luxury in rail travel began to appear in the years after the cessation of hostilities at Appomattox. Passenger travel boomed everywhere in the President Grant era, especially in the Far West, and in a short time evidences of Victorian elegance began appearing in the form of hotel and restaurant cars on the long-distance runs. Shown here in a drawing by A. R. Waud, a noted artist of the Old West, is a Silver Palace Hotel Car as used on the Central Pacific divisions of the Overland Route from Omaha to California. A complete living unit in itself, each of these hotel cars had its own kitchen, staff of servants, and compartments with berths and toilet facilities to insure privacy for its occupants. They were heated, somewhat unevenly, by stoves at the car ends and hot water was brought in pitchers from the kitchen, but if they lacked modern plumbing and thermostatically controlled temperatures, the steamcars made up in florid ornamentation for what they lacked in convenience. A profusion of Turkey carpets, ball-fringe draperies, rare inlaid woodwork, velvet brocaded furniture, crystal lighting fixtures and colored-glass transoms delighted travelers in the Saratoga trunk and Florida Water age. In remote parts of the West, pioneer settlers gladly paid the extra fare, although they had no occasion to travel, just to ride a few hundred miles aboard these truly palatial conveyances. Menus were in keeping with the decor: rich, sumptuous and ornate. Breakfast wines included champagne and claret. Terrapin from Maryland and oysters from Cape Cod were complemented by antelope and bear steaks, fresh mountain trout, quail, plover and partridge. Twenty-five different entrees were not uncommon on the universal dollar dinner, and in this drawing the artist has incorporated, as an index of splendor, a fresh pineapple, in its time and place the rarest and most costly panache of gastronomic elegance.

MILWAUKEE RR

During the first half of the nineteenth century, inns and taverns
had located along the turnpikes and canal towpaths of a nation
accustomed to travel on horseback, in coaches or aboard the
canalboats, of which those plying the great Erie Canal were by
long odds the most splendid. By the late 'forties, however, it was
apparent that the railroad was here to stay and railroad hotels,
in varying degrees of elegance and proximity to the tracks, were
beginning to appear wherever the steamcars went, which was
shortly going to be everywhere. This photograph, taken in 1879,
shows an engine and train crew of the Southern Minnesota Railway posed for posterity before the famed Stone Hotel of Lanes-
boro, Minnesota. The hotel was built in 1868, the year the railroad, later to become part of the Milwaukee system, was built in
from La Crescent. It cost $52,000 and was a favored resort both
of railroad men and passengers. For two whole generations, hotels
were built handy to the railroad tracks and depots, sometimes as
part of the stations themselves, sometimes under separate ownership but contingent purpose: to house, shelter, sluice and feed the
travelers whom the steamcars set down. Under their roofs flourished all the properties of the time: Gladstone valises and Saratoga
trunks, the sample cases of drummers, the theatrical trunks of
traveling troupes of players; gold Albert watch chains and Prince
Albert frock coats, side whiskers, silk top hats; a dish of cloves
and coffee beans beside the decanters on the bar. America was
on its way, fearfully accoutered, toward far horizons and destinies
unguessed. The humble trackwalker (RIGHT), following his beat
on stormy nights, assured them of safety in their going.

Nobody knows the exact locale of the photograph (BOTTOM OF THE PAGE) discovered, in the files of the New York Central System, but it is, from the internal evidence, from the 'seventies, possibly on the historic Putnam Division, and certainly one of the oldest extant action shots of railroading anywhere. The ornate coach interior (LEFT) is also from the archives of the then New York Central & Hudson River Railroad, but from a slightly earlier period, perhaps the late 'sixties. It had ornate panels along its transoms, depicting pastoral landscapes, presumably from the York State countryside served by the railroad. Together, these two rare photographs admirably portray railroading in an age that now seems of geologic antiquity.

As a Yankee artifact and agency of transport, coeval with the clipper ships that slid down the ways at Mystic and Newburyport, the steam engines that rolled through the American countryside during the early decades of railroading were not only useful, they were beautiful and sometimes ornate beyond any devising of artistry since that time. The elaborately ornamented bicycle-type engine, *Hackensack,* outshopped in the 'fifties for the New York & Hackensack Railway, was typical of its time. Engines were brightly painted, their boilers and running parts in combinations of red, gold, green and blue. Steel tires shone like silver, wheel spokes were finelined in crimson and gold, and crimson scrollwork set off the nameboards on engine and tender. Cabs often boasted Gothic windows, bell hangers were richly floriated, brass candlesticks rode the pilot beam for flags, and the side panels of headlights were illustrated with pastorals or scenes of local or mythological significance. American eagles were painted on sand domes, the Union shield and crossed flags appeared where space allowed. A Michigan short line was famous for the cast-iron colored boy on the pilot beam of its engine, holding a vase which was filled with fresh flowers by the engineer's wife on every run. These fine things were universal until the younger Vanderbilt, angered by the malicious rumor that his personal engine *Vanderbilt* was trimmed in solid gold, ordered all ornaments removed from locomotives of the New York Central. The Central at the time was the standard railroad of the world, and its practices were imitated everywhere with the result that engines universally soon assumed the utilitarian aspect of the balloon stacker shown at the left. Until late in the 'seventies a railroad engine was a thing worth seeing.

In a few remote instances some of the original properties of the primeval railroad of the 1830s survived intact throughout the entire age of steam and only disappeared with steam itself. Such was true of the Mississippi & Alabama Railroad, to which greater space is devoted in an appropriate chapter, but whose operations a century and a quarter after the beginning of steam locomotion might best be described by one of the geologic ages that was also part of its corporate title: Early Mississippian. The fifty- and sixty-pound rails of the M & A, resting on unballasted, hand-hewn ties, reached into the scrub-pine forest of Alabama in a pattern that would have been entirely recognizable at the time when Admiral Raphael Semmes first flew the colors of the Confederacy from a ship of war. Its homemade water tower was of primordial simplicity, and the chore of "wooding-up" the tender was still being performed in the atomic age in the identical ritual manner it had been when Andrew Jackson was in the White House. The French proverb, to the effect that the more things change, the more they are the same, couldn't have been more aptly demonstrated than by the wood-burning Mississippi & Alabama Railroad in the year 1950.

That the wrecks of the period engaged the professional attention of magazine sketch artists, to a somewhat greater degree than they did the editors charged with making up the paper, is suggested by this scene of carnage from the pages of *Harper's Weekly,* in 1861, in which twenty members of the 19th Illinois Infantry, on their way to war over the Ohio & Mississippi Railroad, perished. While the grisly details of the mishap are chronicled at some length, no mention is made of the whereabouts of the catastrophe. It is notable that the locomotive depicted in the accident is a bicycle-type with but a single pair of drivers, a magnificent specimen of which eccentric wheel arrangement is portrayed above in an engine outshopped by Danforth Cooke & Company for the Cumberland Railroad to the obvious enchantment of the two silk-hatted officials inspecting it. While fanciful and fast, these engines lacked the adhesion to give them tractive force and soon passed into the discard in the United States.

The rare old action photograph, taken somewhere along the Erie Railroad in the 'eighties and reproduced above, presents a lyric picture of country travel in the golden noontide of steam. The American Standard Type 4-4-0 locomotive still ruled the rails from coast to coast in passenger service, although more sophisticated wheel arrangements were coming into vogue for special freight and passenger runs; and open platform, wooden coaches, painted the dark mahogany color that gave them the name of "varnish," were the rule in a time innocent of vestibules and not yet dreaming of steel construction. The ornate coach interior (BELOW) is from the fabled Virginia & Truckee Railroad in Nevada, three thousand miles distant from the Erie main line, but it might well have been one of the two coaches in the little Erie train. Shown at the car end are the ice-water tank and conductor's wall desk of approved usage, while somewhere behind the photographer was the cannonball stove. The light fixtures on the V & T were serviced with coal oil, although by this time Pinsch gas fixtures were in use on Eastern roads. The ceilings were lined with heavy oilcloth, richly painted in geometric designs of red, green and gold, and the baggage racks above the seats appealed more to the esthetic senses than to practicality. They held little, and what they did hold fell with lamentable regularity onto the heads beneath.

[25]

Way Down East

WILLIAM D. MIDDLETON

The hallmark of New England railroading in the century and a quarter of steam and of its practice in the adjacent marches and provinces of Canada was diversification. In the beginning, its short hauls from terminal to terminal at Boston, Lowell, Worcester or Providence were of an essentially industrial nature, serving mills and manufactories and outlets to the sea. As the rails reached northward into Vermont and the New Hampshire Grants they assumed an increasingly country aspect, running through green meadows and pasturelands and through old covered bridges along Lake Champlain with overtones of mountain railroading where they sought out narrow passes in the White Mountains. At length operations assumed continental dimensions over long-haul divisions to Montreal and Chicago and a now almost-forgotten route that connected Portland directly with Chicago over the rails of the St. Johnsbury & Lake Champlain with Pullmans and diners and plush and ormolu—all too briefly. And always there was the presence of winter, the hard, frozen New England and Canadian winter that froze switches on the Fitchburg, the Old Colony and the Grand Trunk with gelid impartiality. The names of the little lines that were the beginnings of New England railroading are mostly gone now, absorbed in the economy of the Boston & Maine, the New Haven and the New York Central, but legend still remembers the Norwich & Worcester, the Central New England, the Portland, Saco & Portsmouth, the Old Colony and the New London, Northern & Amherst & Belchertown. At the top of this page, a radiant portrait of a classic New Haven 4-4-0 in the 'eighties keeps green the memory of capped stacks and square steam chests. On the page opposite, at the top, a breakdown on the Fitchburg in the 'eighties finds nature lovers among the passengers admiring the river vista, a sketch artist in long linen duster amusing his fellow travelers, and the Yankee merchant, his silk hat pushed far back on his head, smoking a twofer in the contemplation of shrewd trade practices against his rivals. In an age of country self-sufficiency the break is soon repaired and all are off again for Boston town. BELOW: at White River Junction, Vermont, recalled by an earlier generation of New England travelers for the particularly powerful checkerberry candies sold at the depot newsstand in miniature railroad lanterns, the Central Vermont's crack Ambassador on the Montreal-New York run rolls over the White River itself behind 4-8-2 No. 601 for its portrait by William D. Middleton.

The Lay of the Lost Traveler

Hon. Edward J. Phelps, who wrote the following poem, was born in Middlebury, Vt., July 11, 1822, graduated from Middlebury College in 1840, studied law at Yale, was admitted to the Vermont Bar in 1843 and was at one time a law partner of Hon. Lucius E. Chittenden, Registrar of the Treasury during the Civil War. President Millard Fillmore appointed Mr. Phelps Comptroller of the Currency and he served through his administration. Later on he was a Professor at the Yale School of Law, President of the American Bar Association and occupied many positions of prominence in State and Nation; in 1885, he was nominated by President Cleveland and promptly confirmed Minister to England, where he served until January, 1889. The poem is said to have been inspired on an occasion when Mr. Phelps left Burlington by the so-called "Shuttle" train for Boston via Essex Junction. When he got out of this train and stepped inside the Station to await the arrival of the Main Line train, the usual shifting of trains took place and Mr. Phelps without inquiring got aboard a train which he anticipated would take him to his destination, but it was the same train that he had left a few minutes previously and the distinguished traveller found himself enroute back to Burlington his starting point, where, on his arrival, it is stated, this poem was written.

With saddened face and battered hat
   And eye that told of blank despair,
On wooden bench the traveler sat,
   Cursing the fate that brought him there.
"Nine hours," he cried, "we've lingered here
   "With thoughts intent on distant homes,
"Waiting for that delusive train
   "That, always coming, never comes,
"Till weary, worn, distressed, forlorn
   "And paralyzed in every function!
      "I hope in hell his soul may dwell
"Who first invented Essex Junction!

"I've traveled east, I've traveled west,
   "Over mountain, valley, plain and river,
"Midst whirlwind's wrath and tempest's blast,
   "Through railroad's crash and steamboat's shiver,
"And faith and courage faltered not,
   "Nor strength gave way nor hope was shaken,
"Until I reached this dismal spot.
   "Of man accursed, of God, forsaken!
"Where strange, new forms of misery
   "Assail men's souls without compunction,
      "And I hope in hell his soul may dwell
"Who first invented Essex Junction!

"Here Boston waits for Ogdensburg
   "And Ogdensburg for Montreal,
"And late New York tarrieth
   "And Saratoga hindereth all!
"From far Atlantic's wave swept bays
   "To Mississippi's turbid tide,
"All accidents, mishaps, delays,
   "Are gathered here and multiplied!
"Oh! fellow man, avoid this spot
   "As you would plague or Peter Funk shun!
      "And I hope in hell his soul may dwell
"Who first invented Essex Junction!

"And long and late conductors tell
   "Of trains delayed or late or slow,
"Till e'en the very engine's bell
   "Takes up the cry, 'No go! No go!'
"Oh! let me from this hole depart
   "By any route, so 't be a long one"
He cried, with madness in his heart,
   And jumped aboard a train — the wrong one.
And as he vanished in the smoke
   He shouted with redoubled unction,
      "I hope in hell his soul may dwell
"Who first invented Essex Junction."

The long and useful life of the Boston & Main's Class P-4
No. 3713 ended in a blaze of smoke and glory as, carrying white at
its smokebox to show it was running special, it made its final
run over the carrier's Eastern Division in 1956. To achieve this
study in the dramatic rhythm that was the power of steam in motion,
Jim Shaughnessy shot this dramatic photograph with a shutter
aperture of f32 at a speed of 1/50 second as the train was doing
better than a mile a minute. He panned at the exact same speed from
a front 3/4 position as the train came at him at an increasing
acceleration relative to his position, thus blurring the rear of the
locomotive and the background while keeping stack, smokebox and
pilot in precise focus. "It was like a great racehorse looping at full
stride," he said, and froze its motion forever as a remembrance of the
great days that were gone. The scene was a section of the B & M's
double track near Haverhill, Massachusetts.

CHARLES CLEGG

In ever-diminished numbers the covered bridge is still a tangible symbol of New England railroading in the Yankee years, and although steam no longer runs through it, the one (ABOVE) on the St. Johnsbury & Lake Champlain in deepest Vermont may be taken as archetypal of a once universal and still noble example of man's country handicraft at its best. Heading into Chaos and Old Night beyond the headlight beam, the Canadian National's Train No. 15, *The International Limited,* a pool train with cars for Toronto and Chicago, rumbles into the Canadian winter evening at Cobourg where zero temperatures accentuate the semistream-lined profile of a C N 4-8-2. On the page opposite, at the top, is a high-wheeled B & M Mogul of the 'seventies suggesting that all Moguls were not designed for freight opera-tions. *The White Train* (CENTER) on the Boston-New York run was the glory of the 'nineties over the Air Line Route of the New York & New England Railway and was formally known as *The New England Limited.* BELOW: a contemporary of *The White Train* of only slightly less exalted social status takes water from the track pans at Putnam, Connecticut.

JIM SHAUGHNESSY

Before it became the Central New England, the carrier had started out as the Philadelphia, Reading & New England Railroad, and only changed its corporate title, along with its management, in the mid-'nineties. While it was still the P.R. & N.E., the minor contretemps depicted at the left took place when No. 7 proved too heavy for the trestle in front of Richards' Hardware factory at West Winsted. Nobody was hurt. In the below frame, in the year 1890, the P.R. & N.E.'s No. 32 pauses at the depot at New Hartford, Connecticut. The straight barrel of its boiler, square steam chests and austere stack were typical of the utilitarian freight locomotive of its time, as was the derby of the engineer and the curved crossing warning half hidden by its bell and steam dome. The rail under its drivers couldn't have topped sixty pounds.

TWO PHOTOS: GEORGE PHELPS COLLECTION

SUMMER IDYLL IN OLD NEW ENGLAND

COLLECTION OF LEE BEAUJON

In the year 1890, when its high bridge across the Hudson River at Poughkeepsie was one of the wonders of the railroad world, the main-line trackage of the Central New England Railway extended 146 miles through the Connecticut countryside and mid-state New York from Hartford to Maybrook Junction, New Jersey. No railroad to lay claim to continental destinies, it was part of the modest complex of local carriers which included the Housatonic, the Connecticut Western, the Danbury & Norwalk and the New Haven, Derby & Ansonia, all of which were eventually absorbed in the New York, New Haven & Hartford system. In its prosperous 'nineties, however, the C N E ran proud little trains, and the proudest of all was *The Day Express,* shown two pages over, between Boston and Harrisburg, Pennsylvania, via its own line and its connections, the Boston & Maine, the New Haven, the Lehigh & Hudson and the Philadelphia & Reading. *The Day Express* carried the mails, coaches and a fine Pullman Buffet Parlor Car, aboard which prudent Yankee travelers may have been presumed to fare well at lunch (about Winsted) and dinner (about Belvidere, N. J.) off food provided the road by S.S. Pierce, the princely firm of grocers in Copley Square, Boston. Shown above sometime after the turn of the century is the local afternoon passenger leaving Winsted for Norfolk, Connecticut. It is from the collection of Lee Beaujon and represents a rarely photographed phase of New England travel before the coming of the internal combustion.

Whether the Central New England should belong, in geographic assignment, to the Down East of its corporate name, or the Pennsylvania Dutch category of its southern terminal, is a matter of choice. From Boston to Poughkeepsie, 240 miles of its main line and connections were east of the Hudson River, while 224 miles of its New Jersey and Pennsylvania connections between the Hudson River and Harrisburg were west of it. Its rustic operations were a part of the nineteenth-century profile of railroading rather than of the twentieth century, and in the 1920s it was well and unfavorably known in Simsbury, Winsted and Boston Corners as perhaps the worst-managed railroad in the entire universe. Once gone, however, its name retains a certain wistful fragrance as of all vanished yesterdays, and its pictured likenesses are among the rarest of railroad photographs. (ABOVE) *The Mountain Express* leaves Winsted, eastbound, for Hartford in 1890. (BELOW) the baggage room at Canaan, Connecticut, might serve as the model of all the baggage rooms in the world in the years of the Saratoga trunk and Gladstone valise.

Having achieved Northampton, Massachusetts, over the tracks of the Boston & Maine, the Central New England's *Day Express* departed on the sixteen-mile run to Hartford over the right of way of the New Haven, its mail, baggage, coaches and Pullman Buffet behind a capped-stack New Haven thoroughbred such as No. 43 at the bottom of the page, or No. 21 at the left, both classic American Standard 4-4-0 engines of great beauty and pride, embodied in brass candlesticks on the pilot beam, mudguards over the drivers and burnished cylinder heads in the great tradition. In the days when it was earning a cool four per cent every quarter for stockholders in Beacon Street and Dedham, the New Haven was celebrated for its stylish operations and radiant locomotives.

"THERE ISN'T A TRAIN I WOULDN'T TAKE,
NO MATTER WHERE IT'S GOING."
Edna St. Vincent Millay

WILLIAM D. MIDDLETON

Night on the Canadian Pacific finds C P No. 970, a 4-6-0 of austere dimensions, with steam up at Sutton, Quebec Province, ready for the run to Waterloo and back. At ten below, the depot thermometer suggests to the crew the expedient of loading the pilot bar with firewood destined for the crew's quarters at the far end of the snow-filled yard. BELOW: on the superbly pastoral St. Johnsbury & Lake Champlain, an eastbound mixed comes into Morrisville Station from Swanton for St. Johnsbury as a special troop movement, double-headed, stands in the clear to let it pass. All the engines involved are ex-Boston & Maine 2-8-0s. On the page opposite, the northbound *Green Mountain Limited*, on the Boston-Montreal daylight run, is taken over from the Boston & Maine at Bellows Falls by Rutland No. 85, a superlatively groomed Pacific, to pass the Rutland roundhouse drowsing behind a placid New England millpond. In the distance the contours of the Green Mountains give character to the locale and a name to the train they overshadow.

JIM SHAUGHNESSY

RAIL PHOTOS: W. G. FANCHER

RAILROAD PHOTOGRAPHS: H. W. PONTIN

It was the Boston & Albany, when it was first opened to traffic as the Western Railroad in January 1842, that first gave New England merchants and manufacturers, who then dominated the national economy, big ideas of railroading. Although New England was the mother of rail transport in America, carriers had hitherto been built to link only such cities as Boston and Lowell or Boston and Providence, and the idea of serving entire regions through continued and connecting lines and interchange had not been evolved. Rail transport was still strictly parochial. But Albany was the entrepôt for all of Upper York State and the regions coming to be known as the Western Reserve. It offered not static but ever-expanding markets. The Western Railroad was inaugurated, according to the happy custom of the time, with a monster railroad celebration which exhausted cellars all along the line and left celebrants at its terminals palsied and twitching from three solid days of oratory and Medford rum. The road had been built by George W. Whistler, the ranking railroad engineer of his age and father of James McNeill Whistler, and its grades over the Berkshires were miracles of their time. A whole Western world suddenly opened to Yankee imagination, and by May of 1842 trains "of sixty-eight burthen cars" were passing through Springfield and Worcester loaded with cattle, pigs, wool, shingles, whale oil and other merchandise perishable and durable. BELOW: the Boston section of *The Twentieth Century Limited* rolls through Allston in the days when the engines still carried the insigne of the B & A and before the New York Central took away even that dignity of title. On the page opposite, with three ten-wheelers on the head end the Canadian Pacific coaxes seventy merchandise cars up Newport Hill in Vermont, in *The Newsboy,* so called because much of its traffic is in newsprint for the publishing houses of New England.

LUCIUS BEEBE

One of the most spectacular steam engines ever outshopped was the Canadian Pacific's sensational Jubilee Class 4-4-4, shown on the page opposite, flashing across the Canadian landscape on the north shore of the St. Lawrence between Montreal and Quebec City. At the bottom of the page, framed in the doorway of the honored old trainshed at St. Albans, Vermont, Canadian National's 4-8-4 No. 6208 waits a highball to clear the yards for White River Junction on a daytime passenger haul. At St. Albans a highball means just that, as trains are to this very day governed by a ball and halyard fixed to a high gallows arm, the oldest of all forms of railroad signal. On this page, Canadian Pacific's Train No. 41 is being serviced at Brownsville, Maine, on the overnight passenger run from St. John, New Brunswick, to Montreal. No. 2402 takes its train the entire distance of 600 miles from terminal to terminal. BELOW: a Canadian Pacific double-shotted manifest blasts its way through Cookshire, Quebec Province, with merchandise for West St. John, New Brunswick. A pillar of cloud in the heavens salutes its going, while a ridge of snow between the rails shows where the flanger has passed.

TWO PHOTOS: JIM SHAUGHNESSY

JIM SHAUGHNESSY

The impact on the American imagination of Victorian architecture, with its magnificent mansard roofs, *oeil-de-beouf* windows and sweeping lines, was never better evidenced than by the Central Vermont depot at St. Albans, Vermont, shown above in a radiant night scene by Jim Shaughnessy as train No. 20, *The Washingtonian* pauses on its run from Montreal to the Federal City. In the below photograph, *The Ambassador* recreates its pose by day. Built in 1852, the St. Albans station witnessed the Yankee Exodus that drained the youth of New England with the call of California gold in the 'fifties, and in its trainshed troops embarked a decade later, under a Union banner, during the Civil War. On the page opposite, a local freight of the Central Vermont running between Montpelier and Barre passes a covered bridge of the Barre & Chelsea Railroad, one of the last covered railroad bridges to remain in operation and a nostalgic souvenir of country railroading in a more pastoral and unhurried age.

RAILROADS ARE A COUNTRY THING

JIM SHAUGHNESSY

Dating back to an age of balloon stacks and coal-oil headlamps, the primal simplicity of Yankee operations depicted on these two pages lasted until the final breath of engine smoke was discernible over the profile of the Green Mountains. On the page opposite, the operator at Northfield, Massachusetts, framed by the venerable properties of the country depot, hands up his orders to the engineer of a Central Vermont merchandise haul on its way to New London, Connecticut. Telegraphic train orders came into almost universal practice when another Yankee, Charles Minot, by then general superintendent of the Erie, evolved the technique in 1848. On this page, the pattern of country railroading retains its rugged individualism in the man-power-activated turntable at the end of the Maine Central's run at Groveton, New Hampshire. The lower panel depicts a lamentable occurrence on the Vermont & Massachusetts Railroad in 1856, the details furnished from "an instantaneous photograph by Mr. Moore of Athol."

PHILIP B. HASTINGS

"A light for dead men and dark hours . . . ."

SWINBURNE

JIM SHAUGHNESSY

UP IN THE COLD AND ICY

At Sutton, Quebec Province, the icicles from the eaves of the crew's quarters are real and the thermometer reads ten above zero as the Canadian Pacific's 4-6-0 No. 970, a Class D-10h ten-wheeler, awaits the morning call for its daily round trip run to Waterloo. The date is January 1956, and the storm curtains on the engine cab are welcome protection against the gelid temperatures of the Canadian winter.

JIM SHAUGHNESSY

Here the Central Vermont's No. 707, a ponderous and symmetrical 2-10-4, rolls off the turntable at Brattleboro, Vermont, preparatory to hauling its tonnage on the run to St. Albans and, eventually, the Canadian border. BELOW: a wartime consist shows New York Central power in the form of a Class WW-2 Mikado, running over the Boston & Albany near Webster Junction, Massachusetts, with a B & A 2-8-2 as road engine thundering behind. The 1941 emergency overcame the Central's until then tactful policy of retaining Boston & Albany nameboards on all equipment running into Boston.

RAIL PHOTOS: JOHN W. WILLIAMS

PENNSYLVANIA DUTCH

GORDON S. CROWELL

Pennsylvania is the home of big-time railroading, dominated on the Rand-McNally railroad map by the swirling lines of the Pennsylvania System, New York Central, Erie, Lehigh Valley, Lackawanna, Baltimore & Ohio and the Reading Company. For many years, however, it enjoyed a bright and favorable renown among students of railroading as the home of the sole surviving narrow-gage common carrier operating in the East. Connecting with the main line of the Pennsylvania at Mount Union and running thirty-odd miles into the coal-rich communities of Orbisonia, Rocky Ridge and Alvan, its three-foot engines and rolling stock exerted on the senses the charm peculiar to all diminutive things, and its operations both in passengers and freight (the latter almost entirely in coal) flourished green-bay-tree-like, a wonderment and benison for railroad lovers, long after its like had elsewhere vanished from *The Official Guide* forever. In this photograph the East Broad Top's No. 15 rolls a string of empties into the sunrise near Kimmel, Pennsylvania.

SYLVANIA RR

Easily the Great Mogul of railroads in the regions of its name, proprietor, co-owner, mortgagor, lessor, landlord, inheritor or possessor in fee simple of everything in sight, thundering name in the roll call of legend, carrier of all manner of merchandise and all manner of humans, dominating with the assurance of feudal inheritance even the baronial oriflamme of The Standard Railroad of the World, the Pennsylvania, its operations, properties and implications stagger human imagining. Its name trains, *The Golden Triangle, The Red Arrow, The Gotham Limited, The American, The Federal* are the singing names of an Arthurian chivalry of the high iron. Many knowing travelers believe its *Broadway Limited* is the equal in comfort, cuisine and the tangibles of luxury to anything the opposition can schedule. At the turn of the century, in the consulship of lordly Alexander Cassatt, *The Pennsylvania Limited* shown here wore the knightly panache of an observation platform of almost unendurable splendor. Forty years later, as shown below, *The Spirit of St. Louis,* headed by two of the road's incomparable K-4s Pacifics racing westward over the Ohio tangents, was just about the fastest thing on wheels.

LUCIUS BEEBE

All things to all men, coal road, iron road, business track for high-speed varnish between New York and Philadelphia, Chicago, Pittsburgh and St. Louis, railroad of country traffickings, fast merchandise and less than carload lots, the Pennsylvania, in these two pages, presents various aspects of a diverse personality. Here an old-timer on a Civil War trestle tops a Class T-1 semistreamlined 4-8-4, blasting through the depot at Wernersville, Pennsylvania. Across the split, one of the Pennsy's celebrated Class M-1s moves tonnage in the Buffalo Boxcar Run just after crossing Rockville Bridge at Harrisburg, while below is the smokebox of a completely streamlined Class K-4s Pacific designed for passenger service by Raymond Loewy in the 'thirties. The engineer in its cab is waiting a highball.

RAILROAD PHOTOS: JOHN PICKETT

In 1939, the Lehigh Valley Railroad's *The John Wilkes*, crack varnish haul between Jersey City and Wilkes-Barre, Pennsylvania, looked like this in streamlined steam as it streaked across the New Jersey meadows on an autumn afternoon. BELOW: a red-ball merchandise of the Delaware, Lackawanna & Western Railroad highballs into the sunrise with a mile of high cars on its drawbar on a spring morning in 1938 near Morristown, New Jersey.

TWO PHOTOS: LUCIUS BEEBE

In the mellow year 1889, this tall-domed freight engine with its stylish capped stack of the Belvedere-Delaware Railroad, now a part of the Pennsylvania, atmospherically intrudes upon the tranquillity of the Trenton Canal whose traffic the steamcars have long since eliminated from the regional economy. In the lower photograph, the fireman of a Central Railroad of New Jersey camelback, nearly half a century later, expresses the anachronism of two-cab locomotives in a typical pose in his gangway. Canal, capped stacks, camelbacks, all now are with the snows of yesteryear.

[53]   LUCIUS BEEBE

H. REID

At Grafton, West Virginia, a Baltimore & Ohio smokebox justifies the term in an unposed vignette of sooty splendor, while on the page opposite B & O 2-8-2s No. 4401 and No. 4624 pound across the Susquehanna River at Aiken, Maryland, on the head end of a red-ball manifest in April, 1949, for a classic portrait of a double-header on the march.

H. REID

In the immemorial pose of trainmen everywhere, the crew of a B & O Em-1 assigned as helper, await the down train at Faile's Spur on the Lake Branch in Northern Ohio of a misty summer morning.

Mother of Railroads, the Baltimore & Ohio, whose antecedents reach into the dim beginnings of steam, is caught in three likenesses by the camera of Jim Shaughnessy to stand forever as memorial to the beauty that once was implicit in reciprocating motion. On the page opposite, two B & O 7600 Class 2-8-8-4 Mallets move a complementary 7600 tons of coal through Northern Ohio toward Fairport Harbor on the shores of Lake Erie. They embody 32 driving wheels, 8 cylinders, 234 feet of locomotive producing 230,000 pounds of tractive effort, all framed in the white fence of the Ohio countryside on a hot July afternoon. On this page, the road's 2-8-8-4 No. 7609 is shrouded by the vapors of early evening as it awaits assignment to a night run at the Painesville, Ohio, engine terminal. In the long history of its comings and goings, no railroad in America in the age of steam was more typically American than the B & O, none more closely entwined in war and peace in the annals of a nation perennially on the move.

Split-rail fences lined the railroad's right of way, enginehouses were really round with beehive roofs, the Delaware, Lackawanna & Western's locomotives puffed gentle exhaust through balloon stacks, and railroading was a country thing indeed when the celebrated American artist George Inness painted "The Lackawanna Valley" (PAGE OPPOSITE) in the 'sixties on the canvas now in the National Gallery of Art in Washington. Thomas Carlyle, the English esthete, might have deplored the railroad's coming among the hedgerows of Devonshire, but to Innes its tracks and traffiickings made the countryside the more delightful of aspect and most folk have agreed with him ever since. Below is a view of tractive force in its simplest terms in a Morristown & Erie Railroad switcher. On this page, the Baltimore & Ohio's *National Limited* thunders through the cuts and over the fills of the Maryland countryside under a pillar of cloud to gladden the heart of a photographer. Operating departments might deplore such canopied grandeur, but for a century and a quarter the smoke plume in the sky was the symbol of America on the march.

CHARLES CLEGG

A Summer's Idyll, Long Ago

LUCIUS BEE

The Reading Company's stunning 4-4-0 camelback, No. 44 variously shown here in the Reading trainshed at Philadelphia and on the turntable at Lebanon, Pennsylvania, may be taken as the archetype of this exotic breed of locomotive, which flourished for nearly seventy years in specialty density on railroads such as the Reading, the Central of New Jersey and the New York, Ontario & Western. Its mahogany cab, brass candlesticks, square headlamp and massive cylinders and steam chests mark its aristocratic breeding. It was outshopped by Baldwin in June 1888 and served the Reading faithfully until 1921 when it was destroyed by fire. In its days of steam the Bellefonte Central (PAGE OPPOSITE) in deepest Pennsylvania, running eighteen miles between its Pennsylvania Railroad connection at Bellefonte and the academic town of State College, presents, as it rolls up the curved grade into State College, a classic profile of country railroading in the homely short-line manner. Now the last camelback has made its last run and the Bellefonte Central is lost to the splendor of steam, but the memory of their going and glory will outlast the motive power that replaced them.

TWO PHOTOS: THE READING CO.

L. G. HARPEL.

L. G. HARPEL.

L. C. HARPEL

A fine turnout of bowler hats converged (PAGE OPPOSITE) on the Philadelphia & Reading platform at Reading, Pennsylvania, in the winter of 1900, as the road prepared to battle the elements with six other engines coupled behind a typical Reading camelback mounting a huge wedge plow. In the lower photograph, two Reading camelbacks served to get a three-car train on the road out of Lebanon the same winter. On this page, the Reading's archetypal camelback No. 356 halts for the mail and express at Lebanon in the summer of 1895, while (BELOW) the Cornwall Railroad's beloved engine, *Penryn,* pauses of a summer's afternoon at the station of its own name in that now-distant year.

Back in 1895, when L. G. Harpel of Lebanon took this stunning photograph of old-time railroading, the Cornwall Railroad ran five daily passenger trains from Lebanon, Pennsylvania, to Mount Hope, a distance of twelve miles, and three of these went on another nineteen miles to Columbia over the rails of the Reading & Columbia Railroad. On the way it passed Penryn Park, favored of Sunday schools for their annual picnics, and the baronial estate of Peter Grubb, a local magnate, hard by the tracks at Mount Hope. Gentlefolk who wished to avoid contact with the rough workingmen who often peopled the coaches in this coal-mining and steel-manufacturing part of the world, rode in aloof and ornate grandeur in a parlor car such as that shown at the right. Today's brakeman surveying his cut of cars (OPPOSITE PAGE) never even knew the time when gentlemen in silk top hats and ladies in Queen Mary bonnets read *The Lebanon Evening Independent* by the gentle glow of Pinsch lamps on their occasions and business in the Pennsylvania countryside. The railroad is owned by the mighty Bethlehem Steel Company and is operated for freight only, serving the Bethlehem-Cuba Iron Mines Company at Cornwall. The photograph of No. 14 and its spick-and-span two-car train was taken in the early 'twenties when passenger service was still a pleasant and even profitable reality.

[64]

At the Lebanon end of its line, the Cornwall shared the depot of the Philadelphia & Reading, but at Penryn (ABOVE) it set these picnickers down under its own canopy about 1910, while (BELOW) its beautifully maintained engine *Penryn* rolls up to the kerosene-lit platform of the station at Miner's Village in a perfect vignette of travel in the year 1905.

At Mount Gretna, Pennsylvania, just south of Cornwall, was located Mount Gretna Park which boasted (PAGE OPPOSITE) a narrowgage scenic railroad from the Pinch Road at Mount Gretna to a point known as Governor Dick on the adjacent mountainside. At the end of a day under the summer Pennsylvania sky, the country pilgrims boarded a two-car local hauled by stylish No. 10, as shown below at Cornwall Station, for the ride back to Lebanon and the city.

Sleeping cars appeared early on the American railroading scene, a sort of Early Ordovician "car intended for night occupancy" having been scheduled on the Cumberland Valley's Baltimore-Philadelphia run in 1838. By 1843, such was the swift course of progress, two sleepers named *Ontario* and *Erie,* were in long-haul travel on the Erie, where stationary frames of daytime seats provided a sort of couch when made up for night use. The management provided no bedclothes, and passengers went to bed with their boots on. A few years later travelers were delighted to find both blankets and pillows on the New York Central. The drawing below depicting a scene on one of the Erie's sleepers was probably executed some years later, since it shows bedclothes as well as partitions and aisle curtains, but the fair sex, as women were at that time designated, were understandably embarrassed by the prospect of disrobing in the aisle in a wilderness of galluses and congress gaiters. Compared to the compartment cars in vogue in England and on the Continent, foreigners found American sleeping cars an abomination in their lack of privacy, while admitting that the English custom of assigning men and women passengers to the same compartment offered incomparable opportunities for blackmail. By means of a conductor's bell cord, English lady passengers for years made a practice of summoning train crews to their assistance and pointing to disheveled attire to testify to the dastardly intentions of male traveling companions. Classic answer to such accusations was that of a tranquil Englishman who, when accused by a compartment companion of attempted rape, merely pointed to the four-inch ash on his seegar and went on reading *The Times.* The open-berth Pullman sleeper was for more than a century destined to be a standard, durable property of American folklore, legend and a staple of music-hall humor.

& o Blue Ridge Limited 1938

GREEN AISLES

Green aisles of Pullman cars
Soothe me like trees
Woven in old tapestries.
I love to watch the stars
Remote above the earth
In watery light,
While in a lower berth,
I whirl through night.

I love the mysteries
Others abhor:
From Upper Eight, a sneeze,—
That stertorous snore
Far down the aisle. I love
The net of green
That holds like treasure-trove
My clothes unclean.

Cherrywood spick and span
And patterned plush;
The rumble and the rush;

The blankets thick and tan,
All these my heart delight,—
The globe you click,—
Bells ringing in the night
When someone's sick.

Weird bumpings in the night,
Arrivals late
Where stations blaze with light
And bang with freight;
Elf lanterns down the track,
Dark flitting forms
Under a pale cloud-wrack,—
Each aspect charms!

I love to smoke a last
Slow cigarette
Where all ere breaking fast
Ablute and fret;
Then, as on wings of chance,
I plunge the night—
Pullmans, you spell romance
And snug delight!

William Rose Benét

(From THE BOWLING GREEN
An anthology of verse,
selected by Christopher Morley.
Doubleday, Page, 1924)

Among other aspects of American life which were a preoccupation of the distinguished artist, Reginald Marsh, was steam railroading. His favorite railroad, if the number of pictures he devoted to it may be taken as an index, was the Erie. On these two pages, published by permission of his widow, Mrs. Felicia Marsh, and his executor, former-Senator William Benton, are two etchings of Erie locomotives, taking water and at speed, and the cartoon or preliminary sketch of an etching that was never completed. All of them are from the collection of the Museum of the City of New York and supplied through the courtesy of that admirable repository of Manhattan's storied yesterdays.

REGINALD MARSH

On Thomas Grade, Western Maryland's No. 837 head-pins a long drag of coal hoppers en route to tidewater at Baltimore, while below, in an action photograph of salon shading, two 2-8-0s in wide-open action serve as helpers in the middle of the same tonnage train as they hammer up the gorge.

H. REID

RAIL PHOTOS: G. C. COREY

Photogenic beyond most, the Western Maryland, a coal-haul road with access to tidewater at Baltimore, was long a favorite with railroad artists and photographers. Its motive power was unmistakable from its forthright nameboards, and in the above study H. Reid has caught Consolidation No. 849 on a turntable deep in the coal hills at Elkins, West Virginia, as the crew await their assignment. BELOW: three Consolidations in mid-train push a long revenue drag over Thomas Grade with one more at the head end and two at the rear in a dramatic sequence of motive power in tandem with throttles wide open and reverse gears locked in the company notch as they pound up the business track eastbound.

[73]

JOSEPH PENNELL

On the page opposite, the celebrated American artist, Joseph Pennell, drew the Pennsylvania's yards and switching operations outside the Broad Street Station as they appeared after dark in the Philadelphia 'nineties. On this, the Delaware, Lackawanna & Western's last ordered steam locomotive No. 1155, a symmetrical 4-8-4 works the head end of the *New York Express* westbound out of the suburban depot at Brick Church, New Jersey, in 1940, for a handsome portrait of the glory that was steam by Robert LeMassena. Five of these splendid engines once operated in passenger service east of Buffalo where, on the long tangents, they effortlessly topped eighty miles an hour with seventeen cars on their drawbar. In the square below a Pennsylvania 2-8-0 whose footboards proclaim it more appropriate to yarding, ventures briefly into the main near York with a cut of cars ranged, shoemaker-style, with the caboose in front.

LOOK AWAY, DIXIE LAND

From its earliest beginnings, railroading in the Deep South reflected the character of the region it served in that it was archaic, feudal, individualistic and at times eccentric. The first Negro ashcat on record sat on the safety valve of the South's first successful locomotive, *The Best Friend of Charleston,* until the first boiler explosion eliminated both of them, and it was on the locomotives of the Southern Railway that such personalized touches as its radiant green and gold livery, brass candlesticks on the smokebox and spread eagles in bronze survived until the universal doomsday of Diesel. In much the same way that the standard gage of English and, later, American tracks was established by the distance between the wheels of Roman chariots on the English roads, medieval feudalism helped set the style and pattern of Southern railroading. The institutions of landholding and the merging of public and private law in a feudal system of interlocking obligations between landholder and landlord had close parallels in the ante-bellum South and after the War Between the States many parts of the South clung to this unreconstructed economy in an effort to resist Northern dominance and the industrial age it represented. As the most effective vehicle of industrialization, the railroads were feared and hated by the planter aristocracy, and in many instances these influential men were able to prevent the building of carriers into their ancestral domains so that the tracks were forced to bypass communities which in a few years found continued economic existence impossible without them. The result was the construction of a vast and intricate pattern of short independent lines to connect the once-haughty but now-humbled dissident communities with the main-line carriers. In time large numbers of these were absorbed into the far-flung systems of the Southern, the Louisville & Nashville, the Gulf, Mobile & Ohio and the Central of Georgia. Others became part of the Seaboard Air Line, the Illinois Central and the Atlantic Coast Line, but enough survived to give character and individuality to the region until after the Second World War. Until the end, beauty rode the side rods of the Sylvania Central, and as late as 1957, undaunted by time and untarnished by the shabby frauds of progress, the three-foot gage locomotives of the Argent Lumber Company in South Carolina fired their boilers with pine and resin, and their smoke rose through cabbage stacks that were a heraldic device of nobility. A wonderment and a splendor was at the throttle until the end. On the page opposite, H. Reid's photographic study of a faithful servant of the Norfork & Western entitled "The Old Lantern Trimmer" captures much of the spirit of Deep South railroading, while at the top of this page a mission of urgency sends a one-car red ball hightailing through the tobacco fields on the Georgia Railroad in the year 1945.

Bread and Cheese Railroads of the Deep South

Over the twenty miles of Georgia countryside between Wadley and Swainsboro the right of way of the Wadley Southern Railroad resembles nothing so much as a giant roller coaster as its tracks undulate through the scrub-pine woods between Greenway, Blundale and Dellwood. At Swainsboro its daily mixed connected with the equivalent train of the Georgia & Florida in a scene of country simplicity of operations that was out of one of Sheldon Pennoyer's back-country pastorals of the eighteen forties. BELOW: H. Reid has caught a Wadley Southern fireboy scooping the black diamonds through butterfly doors in a pattern of light and motion as old as the first locomotives built to run on hard fuel instead of the cordwood of an earlier practice.

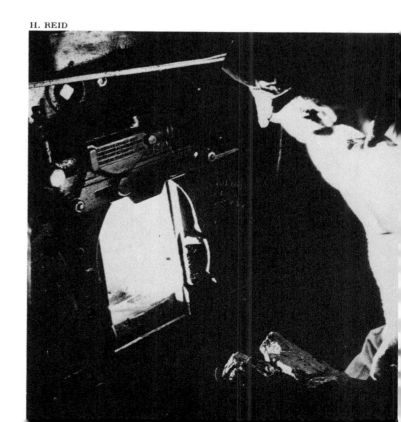

In the highly individualistic, at times even eccentric pattern of short-line operations in the South, the Buffalo Creek & Gauley (which maintained passenger service through the medium of a Mack rail bus), remained in steam well into 1957. The B. C. & G., whose No. 3 is shown above while its crew takes time for lunch at Widen, West Virginia, serves the coal mines of the Elk River Coal & Lumber Company and daily affirms its faith in valve gear, side rods and all the creed of steam. The Jim Crow combine of the Wrightsville & Tennille in Georgia (BELOW) was a surviving trace of the simplicity of operations which for decades characterized little railroads to country places in the Deep South.

Running from Hope Mills to Lumberton—names symbolic of its considerable traffickings in timber, tobacco and cotton—the Virginia & Carolina Southern presented a rich façade of archaism against a background of industrial modernity. Its beautiful capped-stack locomotives recalled the once universal splendors of steam; the countryside through which it ran was out of an American pastoral by Innes, but its purposes and operations were strictly functional and dictated by economic expediency. Its right of way ran here through luxuriant tobacco plantations, there under the green boughs of arching trees, again through meadowlands where its ties and tracks were scarcely discernible from the good brown earth that supported them. Its trestles spanned the sinister waters of Southern bayous. Its sixty-eight miles of light iron through Tar Heel, Tobermory and Bee Gee for interchange with the Atlantic Coast Line and Seaboard Air (as shown on this and the opposite page), were the stuff of heady lyrics in terms of steam, coal smoke and the compelling wonderment of the revolving wheel.

E OPPOSITE: CHARLES CLEGG

LUCIUS BEEBE

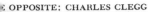

The scene in the Galveston yards of the Houston & Galveston Central Railroad, in 1885, suggests the importance of cotton in the economy of carriers in the Deep South toward the end of last century. Already the steamcars had taken the greater part of the cotton traffic away from the lordly river packets. The tall crenelated stacks moving majestically across the Mississippi horizon were fewer every year, and Mark Twain was lamenting the fate of the woodcutter whose occupational calling along the banks of the Red, the Yazoo and the Ohio was disappearing with the river trade itself. The race of Mississippi pilots was being retired to barrooms in New Orleans and Memphis and, like the cotton itself, the river gamblers were taking their fine linen, tile hats and vest-pocket derringers to the steamcars. It was a time for searching of souls along the water fronts of Natchez, Cincinnati and Maysville.

Even as consequential a carrier as the far-flung Louisville & Nashville, the Old Reliable, once ran mixed trains in steam to the greater glory of God and the picture record. Here in the mid-'forties light Consolidation No. 1308 runs the daily mixed from Barbourville to Manchester, Kentucky, trailing a coach and combine behind its head-end revenue under a gratifying canopy of soot.

Archetypal Arkansas Traveler of a rural countryside, the morning mixed of the Prescott & Northwestern sets out (TOP OF THIS PAGE) from Deaneyville on its rustic occasions for Tokyo and Highland and the great world outside via its mainline connection with the Kansas City Southern. BELOW: for all its imposing title, the unballasted rails of the Georgia, Ashburn, Sylvester & Camilla Railway, when its No. 101 was photographed in 1946, ran a precarious fifty miles from Ashburn to Camilla as part of the short-line empire of the Pidcock family of Moultrie, Georgia. Until the coming of Diesel, Georgia, more than any other region of the Deep South, was the stronghold of a feudal barony of short lines which ran in florid and wonderful profusion through its scrub pine to lend character and meaning to travel.

[83]

SOUTHERN RAILWAY

The flashing green and gold livery of the Southern Railway and its reputation at the turn of the century as a fast-operating line (today its speeds are esteemed only moderate compared to such highball outfits as the Santa Fe and the Milwaukee), gave birth in 1903 to the ballad which, next to "Casey Jones," must rank as the foremost railroading contribution to American folklore. On September 27 of that year, the Southern's train No. 97, *The Fast Mail,* with Engineer Joseph A. Broady at the throttle, was an hour late out of Monroe, Virginia, and Broady promised, as the song later had it, "to put her into Spencer on time." Spencer was the next stop, 166 miles miles down the line. Two firemen were pouring on the coal as the Southern's engine No. 1102 hit the curve leading into Stillhouse Trestle, high above Cherrystone Creek at Danville, at a highly accelerated speed, although probably not the ninety miles an hour of the subsequent ballad. The train climbed the rails and leaped a full hundred feet clear of the trestle before crashing in the creek bed, as shown in the picture. Five cars followed and burst into flames, and the dead numbered thirteen, including Engineer Broady. The song, written shortly afterward by a local hillbilly named Dave George told the story:

> He was going down hill at ninety miles an hour
> When the whistle broke into a scream.
> He was found in the wreck with his hand on the throttle,
> A-scalded to death with the steam.

Broady's bad end as he was "a-scalded to death with the steam" is shown on the page opposite as it was depicted in a popular periodical shortly after the actual event, and the brave engineer and Old 97 together started the long road to immortality as one of the bright gems in the crown of American ballad lore.

In the photograph below, taken in 1945, the green and gold of the Southern is shown, (Like Sheridan, up from the South at break of day) at the head end of a wartime special headed into Washington as it flashes through a locale reminiscent of earlier battles at Manassas Junction, Virginia. Magnificently maintained in wartime as in peace and to the end of the age of steam, the Southern's classic motive power is represented by a scrupulously burnished 2-8-2 No. 4852.

CHARLES CLEGG

From the Great Lakes to the Gulf, the I C once rolled merchandisers such as this at Chebanse, Illinois, behind symmetrical 4-8-2s like No. 2520. On the opposite page, an older 2-8-2 paused in the shade at Madison, Wisconsin, during its daily round trip over the I C's Freeport, Illinois-Madison branch. No. 2969 was originally built for the Vicksburg, Shreveport & Pacific.

WILLIAM D. MIDDLETON

The names that perfume the epic of the Illinois Central Railroad are the names of history, folklore and of railroading itself. Its beginning was promoted by Stephen A. Douglas through land grants in the United States Senate. The legislation was debated by Thomas H. Benton, Hannibal Hamlin, Henry Clay, John C. Calhoun and Daniel Webster. The bill bringing the railroad into being was finally shaped by Webster and signed by President Millard Fillmore. General George B. McClellan was its chief engineer; Abraham Lincoln, an attorney on its law staff. Samuel Langhorne Clemens, who was shortly to achieve fame as Mark Twain, served his apprenticeship as a Mississippi pilot aboard an Illinois Central Line steam packet. General Grenville M. Dodge and Sir William Van Horn, towering figures among the giants of railroading, figured in its building and operations. John Jacob Astor, Stuyvesant Fish, Edward H. Harriman and Andrew Carnegie reaped rich rewards from it, and the I C has been a powerful economic force in the nation since before the Civil War. All these circumstances and celebrities, however, dwarf beside the fact that John Luther "Casey" Jones was on the Illinois Central payroll when he balled his jack straight into immortality as perhaps the most radiant of all American folk and ballad heroes. When he wrecked the *Cannonball* that misty dawn at Vaughan, Mississippi, in 1900, Casey entered Valhalla still trailing intimations of the Illinois Central, a classic figure of tragedy who atoned for error with his own death while saving the lives of others. At the left, the authors of this book together with Mrs. Jane Brady Jones, the engineer's widow, dedicate the marker at Casey's grave in Jackson, Tennessee.

The Mississippi Central, whose own main line operates over 150 miles of track between Natchez and Hattiesburg, connects in its various traffickings with a complex of main- and short-line carriers which include the Natchez & Southern, the Illinois Central, the Louisiana Midland, the Gulf, Mobile & Ohio, the Southern and the Bonhomie & Hattiesburg Southern, the last of which resounding names is that of a twenty-six-mile haul between Hattiesburg and Beaumont on a five-day-a-week schedule. The Mississippi Central, when this photograph was taken by C. W. Witbeck, still operated a stately American type 4-4-0 locomotive with its bell in the grand manner swung from the smokebox and the high, square steam chests of the great tradition.

Rarely seen nowadays, but once a homely operation which required the carrying of heavy metal-sheathed poles on every switcher in the land, is the old-fashioned technique of poling a car into position on an adjacent track. Here shown in practice on the Gulf & Eastern Railroad at Shiloh, Louisiana. BELOW: a stately old-time ten-wheeler of the Missouri Pacific pursues its casual affairs near Thibodaux, Louisiana, in 1947.

C. W. WITBECK

LUCIUS BEEBE

Holding up the cars became a fairly widespread source of employment in the South in the years following the Civil War, and this outrage was reported on the Louisville & Nashville near Bowling Green, Kentucky, in 1875. Below the first section of the L & N's No. 75 passes HK Tower at Anchorage, Kentucky, en route from Cincinnati to Louisville behind two 2-8-2 growlers of noble dimensions. The Old Reliable's other main line out of Cincinnati runs to Atlanta.

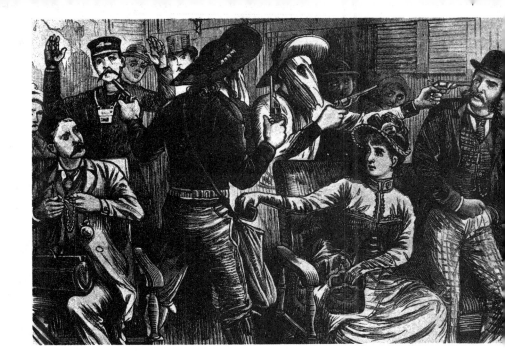

L & N, THE OLD RELIABLE

J. B. FRAVERT

TRUMAN BLASINGAME

Two railroads with roots far buried in the Deep South are here represented in a single locomotive which in happier times had been listed in the motive-power roster of the ancestral Gulf, Mobile & Ohio whose dimensions from the Great Lakes to the Gulf of Mexico had their more modest beginnings in the Old South before the Civil War. When the G M & O succumbed to Diesel, it became No. 603 with the proud lettering of the Georgia & Florida on its tender and is shown here southbound and gleaming from coal boards to silver cylinder heads under the Georgia noontide near Valdosta.

WILLIAM BARHAM

Before the era of giant mergers and consolidations of railroad properties, the essential pattern of the carriers of the South was that of important main lines of continental dimensions fed by a vast network of short lines and branches whose humble trafficking converged in a vast flow of freight and passengers. Prime example of an important main line into the Deep South was the Kansas City Southern whose wartime red-ball manifest was photographed at Neosho, Missouri, as it smoked the summer sky of 1946 behind a 2-8-0 No. 563 and a ponderous Mallet 2-8-8-0, each mounting a cabin for the head brakeman on their Vanderbilt type tenders. On the page opposite, another consequential main-line with its roots far buried in the Deep South is the Gulf, Mobile & Ohio whose 2-8-2 No. 461, with a wartime pay load of sixty-five high cars, thunders southward across the Missouri Pacific crossover at Bixby Tower, Illinois, in 1942. The hallmarks of individuality and character—short-line operations in steam, teapot locomotive and homely traffickings in the ancestral properties of the Deep South, cotton, turpentine, tobacco and hard woods—held out, like the Confederacy itself, until monolithic industrialism and economic pressures eliminated them forever after a last Alamo of internal expansion.

[92]

In this restful scene, H. Reid has perpetuated the memory of the Cliffside Railroad over which, at the very bottom of the state, Cone Mills moves its merchandise in textiles from Cliffside, North Carolina, to market behind demure little No. 110, a 2-6-2 of green cab and bright orange lettering. Its way car with side door and hatted chimney is as individualistic as its engine, and the year, praise God, was as late as 1947.

The four photographs on these pages were all taken by Walter Thrall in the closing years of steam on the Southern Railway System and may be taken as typical of the green and gold individualism of a mighty operation which maintained its character and even a flair for eccentricity to the last. At the bottom of this page, the smoke and glory of the Southern's four and a half per cent grade at Saluda, North Carolina, is embodied in Mallet No. 4056, a 2-8-8-2 as it makes six miles an hour above No. 1 safety track with a 2-10-2 at the rear as helper. At the top of the page opposite, a sister engine heads a similar consist up the same stormy stretch of track, a Silurian multipede framed against the lush vegetation of Carolina hills. At the right, a radiantly maintained green and gold Pacific, flying green from its smokebox, departs Ivy Hill roundhouse in Washington with cylinder cocks open for an appointment with a southbound extra section at Union Station.

FOUR PHOTOS: WALTER THR

When No. 3783, a wonderful high-wheeled 4-4-0, was photographed at Selma, Alabama, in 1938, its simplicity of side rods, wooden pilot beam, tall stack and square steam chests were the most venerable in the entire Southern Railway, having been out-shopped for a now almost forgotten subsidiary in 1885.

Operating for freight only deep in the Louisiana heartland, the Louisiana & Northwest's foursquare No. 37 possessed character and individuality by virtue of a tremendous headlight low on its smokebox, ample staircases reaching from pilot beam to catwalk and an uninhibited volume of smoke exhaust as it blasts out of Gibbsland where it connects with the Yazoo & Mississippi. On the page opposite the Tremont & Gulf's No. 20 made known its early morning presence on the run from Winfield, Louisiana to Tremont where it, too, connects with the Illinois Central's Yazoo & Mississippi subsidiary. Neither carrier was noted for hiding its light under a bushel.

Pillar of Cloud by Day in the Louisiana Bayous

GORDON S. CROWELL

A Sylvan Scene ...

... a woodie Theatre

Of stateliest view

"Paradise Lo

No short-line railroad in the South sur-
passed in archaic stateliness the goings
amidst the pine stands of Georgia of the
Sylvania Central whose daily mixed behind tall-stacked No. 103 is shown
(PAGE OPPOSITE) returning to Sylvania
town from its morning rendezvous at
Rocky Ford with the Central of Georgia.
On this page, as of 1956, the Argent
Lumber Company near Hardeeville,
South Carolina, still snaked out the logs
behind a variety of three-foot gage
wood-burners, including No. 7, a 2-8-0
of picturesque visage as shown here. A
holdup of the Old Reliable, the Louisville & Nashville near Flomaton, Alabama, prompted the *National Police
Gazette* in far-off New York to run this
drawing (BELOW) in its issue of September 20, 1890, with the query: "Was It
the Rube Barrows Gang?"

[99]

CHARLES CLEGG

This is the pattern of all the little mixed freight and passenger trains which, since the dawn of railroad time, have served the far places and humble destinies of a nation living by the flanged wheel on the steel rail. Drawn upon its useful occasions over the thirty miles of light iron between Knoxville, Tennessee, and Sevierville, by a neat 2-6-0 engine of respectable vintage, it presents a picture of homespun railroading almost unchanged in its essential character since first the daily or tri-weekly mixed became part of rural America. Pictured below is a tall tree-shaded operation of the brief-lived Smithfield (Virginia) Terminal, which made the most it might of a former military saddle-tank engine, less than a mile of streetcar rails and an impromptu pier at Pagan Creek, where a ten-mile barge connection was made with the Chesapeake & Ohio at Newport News. That the ham city's venture was of short duration was mourned by friends who admired the picturesque setting of its right of way.

H. REID

[100]

The noble profile here represented is that of the Bennettsville & Cheraw's No. 1, an ageless ten-wheeler which for more than six decades rolled between the cotton plantations and tobacco fields of Kollocks, Blenheim and Bennettsville in deepest South Carolina. Weeds hide the forty- and fifty-pound iron, almost indiscernible from the elemental mold supporting them, but the B & C's motive power has a mind of its own as was demonstrated when, one peaceful Sunday night in 1952, the *One Spot* took off from its home yards in Bennettsville without benefit of orders or train crew, and puffed tranquilly and alone up the darkened line for a distance of eight miles before being apprehended. A home-going worker, observing the ghostly passing of the light engine without either lights or crossing signals, telephoned the road's master mechanic, who, after an automobile chase in the best cinema manner, boarded the engine as it was puffing through the night. Steam leaking into the cylinders were credited with being the cause of the veteran's informal departure, without engineer or fireboy, upon its truant occasion. The independence of character which threw the usually placid carrier into chaos and confusion is further visible in the engine's proud, tall stack, spindly pilot and Indian mascot mounted on its headlight.

CHARLES CLEGG

THE NOBLEST ROAMER OF THEM ALL

On this page the Louisville & Nashville's big Berkshire No. 1985 fills its tank in a rustic setting at Norton, Virginia, while its local merchandise trails back around the curve from Appalachia. At the top of the page opposite, a deep forest recess at Askewville, North Carolina, is the sylvan setting for the daily progress between Ahoskie and Windsor of No. 100, the *R. F. Slaughter* of The Carolina Southern Railroad. Gently impeded by a roadbed grass-grown to the side rods, No. 100 seldom exceeds a prudent ten miles an hour and, to avoid confusion with any other carrier, its tender carries the grammatical article of its corporate title.

H. REID

H. REID

Below is the Nelson & Albemarle's saddle tank No. 9 at Schuyler in the heart of the Blue Ridge country, where it functions as the only common carrier in the land to use this type of motive power in mixed freight and passenger service.

CHARLES CLEGG

Almost a century after the first train brigades began showering sparks on the American countryside, a few unreconstructed carriers such as Brooks Scanlon Lumber Company (LEFT) at Perry, Florida, and the adjacent Live Oak, Perry & Gulf Railroad were still burning wood fuel gathered from the turpentine-pine woods beside the right of way. The photograph below proves that wooding-up, which most Americans imagined to have vanished with the wild buffalo, still occupied the crew of the Mississippi & Alabama during its daily operations in 1949. Mark Twain was sometimes concerned for the fate of the old-time woodcutter who supplied fuel for the Mississippi river steamers and woodburning locomotives of his youth, but forty years after Clemens' own death wooding-up the engines was still being practiced in remote regions of the Deep South.

C. W. WITBECK

CHARLES CLEGG

LUCIUS BEEBE

Possessed until the· end of its age of resolutely characteristic steam motive power, the Texas & Pacific seethed in 1945 when this photograph was taken a few miles east of Fort Worth with wartime traffic which saw red-ball freight, scheduled passenger hauls and troop specials highballing out of East Texas toward the Western Theater of War within sight of each other's markers. Working steam for a grade in the rolling Texas countryside, this splendid 2-10-4, with its characteristic squared sand dome, is the ultimate expression of the T & P's genius for fine motive power. BELOW: the smokebox of the 4-8-4 assigned to *The Sunshine Special* on its through connection between East Texas and St. Louis via the Missouri Pacific leaves no room for mistaken identity of either train or carrier.

[105]

Last common carrier in the United States to operate on wood fuel was the twenty-seven mile Mississippi & Alabama Railroad, running from Leakesville, Mississippi, to Vinegar Bend, Alabama, where it connected with the main line and Diesel operations of the Gulf, Mobile & Ohio to form an atmospheric study in contrasts between self-reliant yesterday and ineffectual today, since its connecting down train, *The Rebel,* was almost always late, the M & A always on time. At fueling stops, located approximately five miles apart along the railroad's uncertain right of way, its venerable 2-6-2 locomotive paused while husky Negroes performed the timeless ritual of "wooding-up." Wood for the boilers of the M & A was cheap and plentiful, requiring only to be cut and stacked from the scrub pine which bounded its right of way for miles. A collector's-item railroad, the M & A continued its homespun operations through the Second World War, a monument to the immutable quality of simple things and country ways. At the left, a section of M & A track isn't altogether up to American Association of Railroads standards.

C. W. WITBECK

CHARLES CLEGG

The simplicities of engine firing and driving as illustrated by the backhead and cab arrangements of the Mississippi & Alabama's No. 4 antedated Lincoln's first inaugural. A reverse lever, long-armed throttle, main and engine air controls were the limit of the responsibilities of the colored engineer. All the fireboy needed was a strong back to keep tossing in the turpentine knots and enough schooling to read the pressure gage, the latter of which he probably didn't have anyway. No. 4's tender held enough fuel to get to the next wooding-up platform (LEFT) five miles down the line and the stroking of a rabbit's foot, in the absence of more scientific instruments, assured water on the crown sheet until the whole excursion got to Vinegar Bend where there was a water tower.

[107]

A Summer's Idyll, Long Ago

GORDON S. CROWELL

Until the end of the Second World War the railroads of the Deep South, both main-line carriers and short lines, retained to a large degree the diversification and individuality that had long since disappeared in institutionalized uniformity elsewhere. Pearl Harbor gave many a short line a renewed lease on life, on borrowed time to be sure, and saved many an aging Mogul, Prairie and Consolidation on the Seaboard, the Southern and the Frisco from the scrapper's torch. In a few instances, the Mississippi & Alabama Railroad and the logging operations of Brooks Scanlon Lumber Company at Perry, Florida, wood-burning engines survived right into the infamy of Diesel. Mixed trains, running behind high-stepping ten-wheelers of noble line and irreproachable ancestry, carried crowded coaches and combines behind the head-end revenue on the Wadley Southern, the Wrightsville & Tennille, the Sylvania Central and scores of picturesque short-haul lines in outland places. So long as war demanded gasoline and rubber, steam lived splendidly on in a never-never-land of turpentine and jim-crow combines and trestles over dangerous but tranquil bayous. The end of the world came with peace. On the page opposite, a breath of summer breathes over the Emory River Railroad's No. 6940 drifting languidly downgrade near Mahan, Tennessee, to form a pictorial idyll of railroading against a background of woodlands that once knew the butternut homespun of the Confederacy and, before that, the fringed buckskin of the pioneers. On this page, a Negro brakeman gives the go-ahead to Brooks Scanlon's No. 5, a wood-burner from the roster of the adjacent Live Oak, Perry & Gulf, at Perry, Florida. BELOW: the daily mixed of the bridge-line Georgia & Florida runs in steam, in 1946, near Valdosta behind a sturdy ten-wheeler with four-square steam chests and a character all its own.

THREE PHOTOS: LUCIUS BEEBE

Running forty-one miles across the rolling Georgia countryside where its rails occasionally are shaded by live oaks and dip into the "beds of the valleys of Hall" beloved of Sidney Lanier, the Gainesville Midland Railroad is a bridge line between the business tracks of the Southern Railway at Gainesville, the broiler capital of the universe, and the Georgia Railroad and Seaboard Air Line at Athens. The last of the Georgia short lines to run altogether in steam, the Midland held fast to its ancient ways and unreconstructed economic philosophy as late as 1957. On the page opposite, No. 207 pauses at Talmo on its morning down run while its sand dome is filled by a bucket brigade on a plank running to the engine's catwalk and its tender is filled with Kentucky lignite by means of scoop and hand barrow. BELOW: one of the road's Russian decapods has its flues cleaned in the Gainesville shops in an ancient pose of unbuttoned dignity. On this page, the railroad's neat offices in Gainesville and (BELOW) the morning consist to Athens rolls dustily across the Georgia countryside under a July sun.

HUGH M. COMER

The last great movement of the symphony of steam thundered to climactic splendor in the years between 1940 and 1950. With the end in sight, the range of its orchestration was most magnificent, sounding a throat-clutching crescendo of light and movement and percussion, recapturing old themes of prophetic woodwinds and drenching its auditors in a final, penultimate crash of exaltation on the plains and in the high passes before being stilled forever. The soaring banners of exhaust smoke towered for the last time against summer skies, and the rhythm of crossheads and reciprocating siderods flashed in blinding radiance through a stanza of splendor. Then the doors of a thousand roundhouses folded shut; on dune and headland sank the fire. The age was ended and the mightiest measure of all man's music was done. It sounded most hauntingly in the Deep South where these two veteran L-I Mikados of the Nashville, Chattanooga, & St. Louis Railroad, running backward in helper service, hike a southbound freight over Cowan Hill fifty-odd miles northwest of Chattanooga. Hugh Comer's dramatic photograph of action in steam has caught all the identifying hallmarks of N C & St.L individuality: Vanderbilt tenders, flanged stacks, graphited smokeboxes and an over-all character and personality destined for oblivion in the age of internal combustion. On the page opposite, two stately Mikados of the Gainesville Midland pose tranquilly of a summer afternoon in the carrier's yard at Gainesville, Georgia.

GORDON S. CROWELL

Perhaps they dismount at last, by some iron ring in the sky....

"John Brown's Body"

CHARLES CLEGG

GORDON S. CROWELL

ABOVE: the daily southbound freight of the Marianna & Blountstown, in the Indian Summer of steam, heads out of Marianna, Florida, at sunrise on its country occasions of cotton and turpentine. BELOW: the Bonhomie & Hattiesburg Southern's No. 200, disused and discarded, dreams of proud days in main-line traffic in years gone by against a somber stand of pines at Hattiesburg, Mississippi.

The Bonhomie & Hattiesburg Southern rocks a profitable train of high cars across a wooden trestle near New Augusta, Mississippi, en route to its Gulf, Mobile & Ohio connection at Beaumont. The Bonhomie of the short-line's corporate title does not exist on the map of its operations, and its thirty miles of right of way are under the same management as the neighboring Fernwood, Columbia & Gulf, which owns forty-four miles of track. Their joint insertion in *The Official Guide* advises shippers: "Save Time and Money by Missing Bedlam and Confusion."

GORDON S. CROWELL

STEAMCARS TO BONANZA

CHARLES CLEGG

Virginia & Truckee

As was true of the pioneers themselves, the major preoccupation, indeed, almost the only one, of the first railroads in the West, was with the bonanzas of gold and silver which brought the eyes of the world to California with the discoveries of '49. In the eighty years of its useful and well-ordered life in the adjacent hills and meadows of Nevada, at the end of which its last run carried it straight into the Valhalla of steam, the Virginia & Truckee was a railroad whose every aspect was characterized by the superlative. Running between the mines of the fabled Comstock Lode at Virginia City and Reno, where it connected with the Central Pacific, it was generally credited with being the richest short line in the annals of American railroading. Its locomotives and rolling stock were the most scrupulously maintained anywhere in the West; its passengers, the nabobs of a wealthy and swaggering generation; and in its last years it was the most written about, photographed and venerated short line in the world. Too beautiful to be scrapped even by the rapacious inheritors of the Ogden Mills Estate, its priceless Kimball coaches and last engines were sold to Hollywood where they live out a comfortable immortality in celluloid. On the page opposite, No. 26 heads the daily mail and passenger run south from Carson City to Minden in 1946. BELOW: the distinguished Western artist, E. S. Hammack, depicts a scene in Virginia City yards in 1875 as the *Night Express*—whose sleepers from San Francisco regularly carried John Mackay, Jim Fair, Adolph Sutro, the peerless Senator William Morris Stewart and other Lords of Creation—arrives on the Comstock.

E. S. HAMMACK

The year 1875 saw the deep mines of the Comstock at Virginia City and Gold Hill in their most effulgent bonanza creating millionaires by the score, sending Nevada's old bearded Silver Senators to Washington and raising San Francisco to a glittering pinnacle of opulence hitherto unknown to the Western World. In Virginia City the V & T's tracks saw the treasure cars spotted at the doors of the strong rooms of Con-Virginia, Hale & Norcross, Gould & Curry, and a sketch artist for *Leslie's* drew them as they were being loaded under the gaze of vigilant representatives of Wells Fargo, the universal bankers and expressmen to bonanza.

AUTHORS' COLLECTI

The year 1875 also saw the purchase by Superintendent Henry Yerington for the V & T from Baldwin of the fine new locomotive *Inyo*, shown below, in a primeval action shot, entering the outskirts of Reno head-pinning the four-car afternoon train from Carson. More than three quarters of a century later fires still burned under *Inyo's* crown sheet as it played the starred role in the cinema spectacle, "The Great Locomotive Chase."

JOHN ZALAC COLLECTION

More, perhaps, than any railroad in the American legend, the Virginia & Truckee kept faith with the past, maintaining a continuity until the end of its eighty-year life span with the fabled years of bonanzas and the silver nabobs of a splendid generation. It had been built by the all-powerful Bank of California to connect Virginia City with the mills along Carson water and the Central Pacific's transcontinental main line at Reno. For eight decades its comings and goings were a household concern along its country right of way through Washoe Meadows; its passengers, the wealthy and powerful of the earth; its motive power and operations, the wonder and envy of railroad men everywhere. Gilbert Kneiss, official historian of Nevada's short lines, estimated that over the years the V & T carried down from the Comstock in silver bullion and gold the equivalent in weight of its every engine, coach, trestle and length of rail. When the long twilight of the short lines set in during the 'forties of the nineteenth century, No. 27 (ABOVE) was still a glory in Washoe Meadows at sundown with the afternoon mixed from Minden, and minted dollars of Nevada silver were still its regular freight between the banks of Reno and Carson City, as shown below. Until its final run the V & T was the Dollar Princess, the Golden Girl of the short lines.

This Week

THE GOLDEN GIRL OF
AMERICAN RAILROADS

CHARLES CLEG

With No. 26 as helper and No. 27 as road engine, a V & T wartime double-header on the Reno-Carson City run, in 1946, emerges from Washoe Canyon over a business track completely hidden by grass, while a siding is barely perceptible in the foreground growth.

The first car, home-built as a way car in construction service for the V & T at its vast granite shops in Carson City in 1870, was still spotted under the cottonwoods there three quarters of a century later. Its final years saw it freighted with glamor when it was rebuilt as a club car for outings and special excursions and named *Julia Bulette* for Nevada's first and most notable courtesan. The Cyprian had come to a bad end in the Virginia City 'sixties, but the car that carried her name lasted as long as did the railroad itself.

In 1938, the main line of the V & T from Carson City to Virginia City was abandoned and the last of many thousands of highballs sent the last train down the grade from Gold Hill station. Still the depot whose platform had resounded to the boots of the nabobs of the golden years basked in the Nevada sun, its telegraph circuits stilled forever, a repository of splendid memories when the implacable storms of winter swept over the once-populous Washoe Hills.

This home-built wooden tank car was constructed in 1868 in Carson City to take water to track-laying gangs in the desert beyond Empire and was still taking its ease in Carson yards in 1946.

In 1950, the V & T, full of years and honors, rolled its last train, pictured here, across the meadows on the edge of Carson City and over the grade at Lakeview. Of all the heirs of Darius Ogden Mills who had financed the railroad's building, none cared to underwrite its ever-increasing annual deficit, and at length the canyon at Washoe Lake, the hot springs at Steamboat, knew it no more. But while the memory of man runneth, its name will be kept green, perhaps the greatest of all the pioneer railroads whose days had been long and its annals golden in the noontide of the Western land.

LUCIUS BEE

PARAMOUNT PICTURES

The Second World War saw V & T engines No. 25 and 26 still in active service and shown above double-heading a long mixed consist of tanks and four coaches out of Carson City en route to Minden in 1946. At the left is the ornate bell-hanger devised for *Inyo* by Paramount for its appearance in period Westerns. In 1900, Fred Jukes, a boomer railroad man who was to become himself something of a legend in the West, took the photograph on the page opposite, showing the V & T's beautiful Kimball cars in the afternoon varnish run at Carson City, waiting for a highball to whistle off for Empire, Mound House, American Flat, Gold Hill and Virginia City. Like *Inyo*, they were to achieve celluloid immortality in such films as "Union Pacific" and "The Return of Jesse James."

The year 1900, when *Inyo* had already seen a quarter of a century of life and movement among the Nevada bonanzas, found it in this rare old-time photograph clearing Reno yards as it doubled in freight with a string of merchandise cars for Washoe City.

Lake Tahoe in the California-Nevada Sierra is 6,200 feet above sea level, 24 miles long and 1,500 feet deep, and for more than a third of a century was served by the rails of the narrow-gage Lake Tahoe Railway & Navigation Company between Tahoe City and its connection with the Southern Pacific main line at Truckee. It was the project and property of Duane L. Bliss who, in the booming years of the Comstock Lode, had acquired the right of way in Nevada for the Bank of California to build the Virginia & Truckee Railroad. When mining on the Comstock began its long decline, the Carson & Tahoe Lumber & Fluming Company, which Bliss had organized to supply Virginia City with timber, pulled up stakes and built the rail connection with the Southern Pacific, and began operating three passenger trains a day in connection with a lakeside resort at Tahoe City and a fine excursion steamer, *Tahoe*, which plied the nearby waters. The old-time photograph shows the L T R & N's engine No. 1 in 1908 arriving at the pier with excursionists for the *Tahoe*, moored handily alongside. BELOW: the V & T's No. 11, *Reno*, makes its Christmas Day run in 1875 through a snow-powdered Nevada desert, as seen by the artist's eye of E. S. Hammack.

LORY RODE THE WASHOE HILLS WITH NO. 11

Not even excepting the Yankee clipper ships from the drawing board of Donald McKay or the thorough-braced Concord coach of Abbot Downing Company, no devising of human genius for the conquest of time and distance was more beautiful or more useful than the American Standard 4-4-0 steam railroad locomotive. And no single artifact, not even Colonel Samuel Colt's Patent Revolving Pistol, was more an instrument of Manifest Destiny in American continental conquest. For more than a century this wheel arrangement bridged the far places of the nation, and although more sophisticated designs eventually replaced it for special tasks, no engine type was ever so versatile or satisfactory on so great a variety of assignments. The first 4-4-0, the *Blackhawk* was outshopped in Philadelphia in 1836 and was found to be a vast improvement over the single pair of drivers until then in use to provide "traction without wheels sliding." Matthias Baldwin held out against the American for nearly a decade, but in a few years the finest thoroughbred engines in the world were being turned out to this pattern by William Mason of Taunton and the 4-4-0 was the standard product of such builders as Brooks, Cooke Danforth, Rogers, Hinkley & Drury, the Taunton Locomotive Works and Manchester. Now and then the 4-4-0 pattern was adapted to eccentric design such as in the camel-back engines which for many years were characteristic motive power of the Reading, Central of New Jersey and the New York, Ontario & Western lines. The earliest cab-first mallet, built for the North Pacific Coast Railroad, was also a 4-4-0, but, largely, they conformed to the conventional pattern of a horizontal boiler with following cab and tender like the vast majority of all American steam locomotives. The last eight-wheeler was built by Baldwin in 1922 for the Southern Pacific, but on many lines they continued to run until the very end of steam. All Nevada felt that the V & T's No. 11, the *Reno*, shown here at Carson City, outshopped by Baldwin in 1872, was the most beautiful engine in the world and for a full half century it was the most beloved property of a railroad where all the motive power was loved and cherished.

The years of the Virginia & Truckee's great moments and golden destinies were the era of the frock coat, escorts for ladies venturing in public, and other formal proprieties and, with a few notable exceptions, its annals were those of dignity and rectitude. One of the exceptions was the occasion when, in the mid-'eighties, Madame Bentz's Female Minstrels, having finished a stand at Piper's Opera in Virginia City, paused for refreshments at the bar of the Frederick House handy to the tracks while waiting for the night sleeper for San Francisco to be made up. By the time the train was ready for a highball, the girls had given double significance to the phrase, and an unseemly tangle with the train crew took place on the station platform before the company could be gotten on board and bedded down for the night. Darius Ogden Mills down in San Francisco, when confronted with the pictorial record of the episode, reproduced below from *The National Police Gazette,* took a dim view of such unseemly scuffles and ordered Superintendent Yerington to suspend all free theatrical passes over the line until troupers showed evidence of sobriety before boarding the cars. At the right, although no train would ever again follow or a second section be scheduled, markers for the V & T's final run in 1950 were as scrupulously cleaned and lighted as ever they had been in the road's times of teeming commerce. Until the very end the V & T was a carrier of proud ways and irreproachable propriety.

This We

the top of the page, the V & T's No.
purchased from the Nevada Copper
lt when that carrier abandoned oper-
ions, and the last locomotive of the
rginia & Truckee's long and historic
ster of engines, highballs through
ashoe Canyon with the morning mixed
1949. BELOW: the drawing-observa-
n salon of *The Gold Coast,* last of the
ivate cars to call the V & T its home
ilroad, the first having been Superin-
ndent Henry Yerington's business car
often borrowed by Bonanza King
hn Mackay. A particularly spectacular
gregation of private cars rolled over
e V & T tracks from Reno to be spotted
Carson yards in 1897 for the Corbett-
tzsimmons boxfight. They were filled,
cording to *The Carson Appeal,* with
ead-game sports arrayed in purple
d fine linen with well-brushed tiles"
d their resources of luxury, including
iagaras of vintage champagne, left
evada, if not their occupants, breath-
ss.

Green Light To Valhalla

LUCIUS

The last of the sunflower stacks, the last of the old bearded eagle-eyes and throttle artists who had conquered the Great Plains and the high passes, the last of the open-platform coaches and Wells Fargo treasure cars, all were the properties of the Virginia & Truckee, itself the last of the bonanza short lines of the Old West. These photographs, taken in its final days of operations in the Nevada desert, establish a continuity, unbroken in its implications of spacious times and golden destinies, between the year 1950 and the bonanza years that had gone before. On the page opposite, No. 27, fitted with a sunflower stack for its ultimate run, rolls south under a sky-flung canopy of soot past Slide Mountain near Lakeview with the morning passenger and mail haul augmented by the road's single caboose. On this page, High Water Bill Fryk, with his hand on the throttle and his eye on the unending rails ahead, assumes the immemorial pose of the old-time engineer. Recapitulated in his whiskered profile, twofer cigar and squinted gaze is all the smoky legend of railroading in the Old West that had gone before; the pioneers at the reverse levers of primeval teapots, rocking precariously over ungraded roadbeds; the throttle artists of the great tradition, wheeling the *Overland*, the *Sunset* and the *Fast Mail* across the illimitable plains of yesterday. It was the smoke of their first coming over the horizon of the East that fired Joaquin Miller to the sentiment: "There is more poetry in the rush of a single railroad train across the continent than in all the gory story of burning Troy," and the smoke of their going at last saddened many hearts that had known and loved them.

Built to run 300 miles through the Nevada-California deserts as a subsidiary of the Virginia & Truckee and connecting with that line at Mound House near Carson City, the narrow-gage Carson & Colorado Railroad is best remembered for the remark of crusty old Darius Ogden Mills, whose Bank of California had financed the venture, that, to his mind, the road had been built "either 300 miles too long or 300 years too soon." Running southward in Nevada with an eye to the mining prospects of Candelaria, Luning and Basalt, the C & C crossed into the Owens Valley of California via Mt. Montgomery Pass and a vestigial trace remains there to this day as the narrow-gage Owens Valley Branch of the Southern Pacific. In the 'eighties the passenger run from Mound House to Keeler took two days and the little train was known as *The Slim Princess*. On the page opposite are two rare photographs taken in 1883, (ABOVE) near Queen Station at the California-Nevada line and (BELOW) at the south portal of Mt. Montgomery Tunnel. On this page is shown narrow-gage No. 8 near Independence in 1950. BELOW: drummers who traveled aboard *The Slim Princess* in the 'eighties found their ulsters comfortable in the desert night, but skullcaps better adapted to the clearances of the little wooden coaches than the silk tiles of fashionable usage. For a short time after the Tonopah and Goldfield discoveries, the road rolled in unaccustomed prosperity, but over the years its annals were more romantic than rewarding.

The
Slim
Princess

SOUTHERN PACIFIC RR

When the Central Pacific's mixed freig[ht] and passenger train paused for its ph[o]tograph at Mill City, Nevada, sometim[e] in the late 'eighties, the crew were n[ot] the sort to forget the train pet, an[d] Towser is shown in repose on the pil[ot] beam next the bearded fireman. Th[e] action shot (BELOW) was taken in th[e] last years of useful existence of the Ton[o]pah & Goldfield Railroad which co[n]nected those mining towns in the sout[h]ern desert of Nevada with the narro[w] gage Carson & Colorado at Tonop[a] Junction. In the height of the Goldfie[ld] excitements in 1905, its cars were f[a]miliar to the latter-day nabobs of pr[e]cious metals, Tasker Oddie, Key Pi[tt]man, Charles M. Schwab, Bernard B[a]ruch and Montana's acquisitive Senat[or] William Andrews Clark. When the na[r]row-gage C & C was standard-gaged [by] the Southern Pacific, there were throu[gh] Pullmans to San Francisco of rich a[nd] rococo decor. When this photogra[ph] was taken during the Second Wor[ld] War, the T & G was hauling high-octa[ne] gasoline across the desert to an air ba[se] near Tonopah.

SPACIOUS DAYS IN THE NEVADA DESERT

The now-abandoned Nevada Copper Belt which joined the Southern Pacific's Mina Branch at the four corners hamlet of Wabuska furnished this profile of desert railroading during World War II. Its tidy locomotive No. 5, a few years after this picture was taken, was sold to the Virginia & Truckee and served out the life of that historic railroad on the daily run from Reno to Minden via Carson City. The photograph below, in the Stetson-hat-and-fireman's-gallus age of Tonopah, was taken by C. R. Terrell, editor of *The Tonopah Times-Bonanza* and a frontier mining-town newspaperman of six-gun celebrity.

A. SHELDON PENNOYER

The treasure cars of Wells Fargo & Co., clattering at the drawbar of balloon-stacked wood-burners into the foothills of the Mother Lode of California and the Washoes of Nevada, are now one with the bearded prospector and his faithful burro, the assayer and his gold scales that had gone before them. But the sound of their riding is part of the music of the West forever, rising in splendid ghostly allegretto against a background symphony of "Clementine" and the trip hammers of a thousand stamp mills thundering in an eccentric rigadoon of golden recoveries.

Genoa

TWO SONNETS

WALT DISNEY

All night she drifted down the Washoe grade,
A light in dark hours for the souls of men,
A herald of the morning—so they said,
Till morning met her in the meadows, then
Shot through with dawn and gilded with its
    fire,
All red and gold *Genoa* came at last
In smoke and splendor to the heart's desire,
Leaving the spirit singing where she passed.

I shall not see her beauty come again
And much went with her going that was fair:
A certain Western gladness and an air
Of Western loveliness in pass and plain.
There is no beauty such as this today
That went when that fair engine went away.

There was no engine like *Genoa*, none,
No engine like her ever built by man.
Men put their tools aside to see her run,
Lifting their hearts as only engines can.
Of all the mountain mileage she was queen,
An air of royalty contained in going
And all perfection caught in a machine
To clutch the throats of men beyond their
    knowing.

I pity men who never rode a train,
Sensing a purpose in the shining wheel,
The crossheads flashing out and back again
Obedient in a symphony of steel.
And though the track is long since grown
    with grasses
I see a glory where *Genoa* passes.

                                     L.B.

California
The
Golden

ROBERT HALE

LUCIUS BEE

4421

Other transcontinental main lines—the Western Pacific, the Union Pacific and the Atchison, Topeka & Santa Fe—enter California from the east and north, using its metropolises of San Francisco and Los Angeles as terminals and trafficking in the abundance of a golden land, but from earliest times—and probably it will so be until the sun sets forever upon railroading—California has been the feudal property of the far-flung, imperial Southern Pacific Company. Its antecedent carrier, the Central Pacific, made possible the realization of American continental destinies when on that wet and windy day at Promontory, Utah, in 1869, it met the western railhead of the Union Pacific. The Espee's acquisitive overlords and bearded old Kings of Get—Leland Stanford, Collis Huntington, Mark Hopkins and Charles Crocker—were for decades co-owners of everything in sight, ordering the affairs of California as satraps might a province far separated by time and distance from central authority. "We will cave him down the bank," said Huntington when a rival arch-millionaire challenged his authority—and he did just that. On the page opposite, an Espee Class GS 4-8-4 hits eighty southbound out of Tracy with the *San Joaquin Daylight*. On this page, the *Coast Daylight*, "the most beautiful train in the world" in its days of steam, passes through Salinas.

HOWARD FOGG

Austere the Far Traffickings of the Southern Pacific

A. B. FROST

Far-ranging, the operations of the Espee extend from the wintry Cascades of Oregon, represented here by A. B. Frost's lonely trackwalker, to the Arizona desert depicted above by Howard Fogg's splendid double-header in the year 1886, after the Southern Pacific's rails had joined those of the Galveston, Harrisburg & San Antonio to provide through service between California and New Orleans. Ten or a dozen high cars were the tonnage limit for a brace of tall-stacked 2-8-0s over the ruling grade where they make a fine picture against the backdrop of the Old Southwest. On the page opposite, at the top, the eagle-eye lodges his throttle in the company notch as Espee No. 2575, a 2-8-0, gathers speed for the miles with forty cars of way freight running north out of Lathrop, California, while at the bottom of the page, a wartime extra rolls out of Palm Springs behind double-headed power maintained in the great tradition of steam operations.

[139]

HENRY R. GRIFFITHS, JR.

The Southern Pacific had come a far piece between the day when the scene of pastoral railroading was. photographed (PAGE OPPOSITE) in the Sacramento 'eighties and the end of the era of steam when cab-first Mallet No. 4211 posed for a split second for its portrait amid the Nevada sagebrush on the Alturas run. The meeting of the rails in the desert at Promontory Point to span the continent was still dramatically in the public mind when these bearded switchmen stood beside their wood-burning engine while the swing bridge across the Sacramento River showed mistily in the background. Eighty years later the Modoc Division out of Fernley, the Southern Pacific's back door to the Northwest, was one of the last strongholds of steam anywhere in the West where No. 4211 bucked Madelaine Hill with ninety cars on its drawbar. On this page Train No. 51, *The San Joaquin Daylight,* projects a pattern of speed through a warp of communications wires as it hits eighty northwards out of Lathrop.

ROBERT HALE

MAIN LINE NOCTURNE

RICHARD STEINHEIMER

At the top of the page, a Silurian land-creeper, the Sacramento Valley's locomotive, *Lincoln,* poses for its portrait in the misty dawn of California's primeval photographic *expertise* at a water tank in the year 1860. BELOW: in a character portrait taken nearly a century later in the same California mists by Richard Steinheimer, a Southern Pacific trackwalker sets out for his day's round of duty along the fog-shrouded main-line tracks skirting the waters of San Francisco Bay south of the city itself.

On the page opposite, in an atmospheric salon study of night operations by Richard Steinheimer, Southern Pacific's No. 3625 waits, in the hot dark of the California night on Saugus Siding, for the heavy Fillmore local freight to run off the Montalvo Branch on its way to Los Angeles. Breathing deep of the valley air as its crew awaits their assignment, it will boost the merchandise over the short hill into Fernando in an obscure but revealing contribution to the effectiveness of the biggest railroad of all.

[143]

Last of the privately owned and operated railroad cars to call the Southern Pacific its "home" railroad was the Pullman-built *Virginia City*, shown on the page opposite, the property of Charles Clegg and Lucius Beebe. Hailed by the press and widely publicized throughout the world as the most beautiful private car ever outshopped in the history of American railroads, the decor of *The Virginia City* is Venetian baroque designed by Robert Hanley of Hollywood. Fourteen-carat-gold fixtures, gold lamé drapes, crystal chandeliers made to the car's order in Venice and a propane-activated Italian marble fireplace characterize the drawing-observation salon. There are three master staterooms with a shower bath and steam-room, a dining compartment seating six at table, and galley, storage space and crew's quarters for chef and steward. A familiar sight on the private car tracks of the Los Angeles Union Station (RIGHT), *The Virginia City* was also often routed in the middle 'fifties over the Southern Pacific's Sunset Route to New Orleans on which run Train No. 2, *The Sunset Limited*, is shown below in its days of steam operation at Palm Springs, California.

TWO PHOTOGRAPHS: ROBERT H.

SERENE & SYLVAN THE SIERRA ROAD

Beloved in the lifetime of steam for its variety and beauty of motive power uncommon in a short line and picturesquely situated in the heart of California's Mother Lode in the Sierra foothills, the Sierra Railway operates fifty-seven miles of main line from Tuolumne to Oakdale by way of Jamestown, Chinese Camp and Hetch Hetchy Junction. Its diminutive combine shown at the right and the rugged Mallet No. 38 (BELOW) were two reasons why the railroad was in great requisition among Hollywood film companies seeking location shots and the faithful of the rail fans. Excepting only such celebrated short lines as the Virginia & Truckee and the Sumpter Valley, it was probably the most photographed short-haul railroad in the West and the pictures on these pages give some idea of its character and individuality in the golden years.

CHARLES CLEG

ROBERT HALE

ROBERT HALE

CHARLES CLEGG

In a farewell salute to steam before its complete Dieselization, the Sierra ran a final double-header of No. 38 and No. 28, as shown above, from the negative of Robert Hale. Its stately No. 34 against a woodland background was photographed on an earlier and happier occasion.

Named for the California county of its operations, the twelve miles of track of the Amador Central between Ione and Martell contain a hundred curves, a four per cent grade, an elevation rise of 1,100 feet and twelve bridges. It serves a giant lumber mill at Martell and meets the Southern Pacific at its western terminal at Ione. Its daily train on its round trip, when these photographs were taken in 1945, required an hour each way. The railroad came into being in 1906 as the Ione & Eastern, and in early years its major traffic was in ore concentrates coming out from the historic deep mines at Jackson. At the left, its up train is shown behind No. 7, a venerable Prairie type 2-6-2, rounding a steep California hillside on a summer morning. Three loaded high cars are its tonnage limit, and if there are more from the Espee interchange, two round trips to Ione must be made. Its rare teapot locomotive, archaic operations and country ways established, in its days of steam, an unbroken continuity with California's earliest carriers built to serve the Mother Lode in gold-rush times.

Until the abandonment of passenger service between Galt and Ione, the Amador Central maintained a daily passenger run and was a favorite with excursionists and picnickers from San Francisco. In 1945, one of its two coaches still stared through sightless windows into the long vistas of the Mother Lode, prophetic even then of the autumn years of steam.

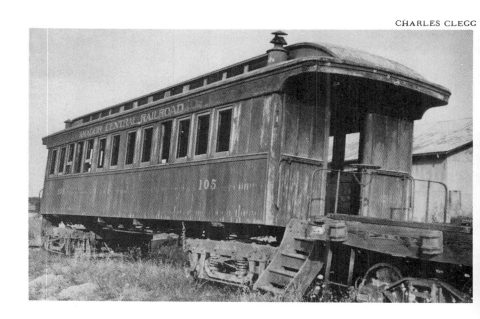

VO PHOTOS: CHARLES CLEGG

A study in the informal railroading of an earlier and less sophisticated era, the Amador's No. 7 clatters across one of the trestles spanning the deep ravines of its right of way. Dutch-oven-like arrangement on pilot shelters a hose reel as protection against fire. At the left, the up-train pauses for water halfway between Ione and Martell. Six miles of steaming have exhausted its tank and required primitive replenishment.

[149]

In this spirited drawing of wood-burning yesterdays, the distinguished railroad artist, E. S. Hammack, has recreated the golden age of steam in a California yards of a carrier unidentified, but in whose corporate title a terminal at Ultima Thule may be imagined. In the foreground the road's business track reaches toward golden destinies beyond far horizons as the morning varnish whistles out of town; on the hand-activated turntable with its wooden gallows frame a Consolidation No. 19 is turned for a freight run into the neighboring Sierra. In the background are roundhouse, foundry, backshops, all the structural resources of operations in a halcyon time when woodsmoke marked tranquil rights of way and the steamcars, on their lawful occasions, served such atmospheric places as Gold Run and Whiskeyville, Hangtown, Pickhandle Gulch and El Dorado. On the page opposite, one of Richard Steinheimer's documentary nighttime photographs shows the Southern Pacific's Mogul No. 1771 switching at El Centro in the Imperial Valley. The hour is midnight; the year 1953.

E. S. HAMMACK

RICHARD STEINHEIMER

On its maiden trip from San Francisco to Los Angeles, in 1949, the Southern Pacific's Train No. 94, *The Starlight,* blazes like a beacon in the California night at the historic depot at Third and Townsend. Beyond its silver smokebox in the dark *The Lark* waits to follow it out of the yards and through the moonlit meadows and mists of the shore-line route to the Southland.

The Yosemite Valley Railroad is now no more than a golden souvenir of California railroading in the days before the motorcar usurped the short-haul tourist trade. It was built in 1907 to run from Merced, where it connected with the Southern Pacific, to El Portal at the edge of Yosemite National Park. Overnight Pullmans from San Francisco, a venerable wooden observation car with galley for light housekeeping and some of the most spectacular scenery in the West were the properties of the Yosemite Valley in its times of teem. In its less than half a century of operations, the railroad never had an accident of serious proportions, and three Presidents of the United States, the last being Franklin Delano Roosevelt, had their private cars routed over its inviting trackage. Here its down-train passes through a deep cut in the California hills a few miles out of Merced. In the silhouette (BELOW) by Robert Hale, two cab-first articulated engines of the Southern Pacific against the setting sun near Roseville symbolize the twilight of steam in its closing years on the greatest of Western carriers.

CHARLES CLEGG

ERT HALE

HIGH SIERRA

When, at the conclusion of the Civil War, the first promoters of the Central Pacific Railroad announced their intention of building to meet the rails of the Union Pacific in a transcontinental main line, political enemies charged that their true purpose was merely to float stock issues on a grandiose scale while actually projecting their line only into the Sierra to tap the wagon trade to Nevada's booming Comstock mines. They called it "The Dutch Flat Swindle," but as the rails passed far beyond Dutch Flat and down the far slope into Nevada and the Humboldt Desert, criticism turned to admiration and the Pacific Railroad became the "Work of the Age" as the Erie Canal had been before it. At last, in 1869, the through run to the East became a reality. Drifting down the long cut six miles west of Gold Run (PAGE OPPOSITE), the train suddenly emerged upon the very rim of the world itself, and the lead engineer whistled for brakes to bring the cars to a pause at Cape Horn. There a half mile below, straight down, was the American River, source and fountainhead of the gold that had turned the eyes of a nation westward; there before them over the misty and receding foothills of the Sierra was California the Golden, the Far Western Land, and finally the blue Pacific. Briefly, as they climbed to the cartops or the edge of the canyon beside the track, the passengers were one with all that had gone before them; the pioneers in Fremont's train, the bullwhackers and jerkline artists, Hank Monk, Prince of Jehus, high on the driver's seat of his pitching Concord, aloof as an earl with mails for Nevada. But mostly, because in their mind's eye they could see the Pacific itself, they thought of Meriwether Lewis and William Clark who, six decades before, when at last they too had achieved the Pacific, wrote in their journal the immortal cry: "Ocian in view! O! The Joy!" Three quarters of a century of steam later, during the Second World War, when every type of motive power on the Southern Pacific's widely various roster was being called into service, William Barham caught an eastbound fruit block highballing out of Roseville on the ever-ascending grade headed by an ancient 2-8-0-of-all-work running as helper and an early series cab-first 2-8-2 Mallet.

WILLIAM BARHAM

E. S. HAMMACK

In the early years of the Central Pacific's operations in the Sierra, while the railroad was still a stub line reaching only to the gold-rush towns of the Mother Lode, the treasure cars (ABOVE) as they carried down the bullion to Sacramento were never molested. Robbing the cars became fashionable only after through service to the East was inaugurated in 1869. When, on the afternoon of November 4, 1870, Train No. 1, predecessor of *The Overland Limited*, headed into the long tangent out of Sacramento (PAGE OPPOSITE) behind a balloon stack of noble dimensions, nobody on board imagined they were riding toward a rendezvous with history. Early the next morning at Verdi, on the Nevada side of the Sierra, No. 1 was held up in the first train robbery in the Far West. The Wells Fargo safe was looted, as shown in this contemporary drawing, of $41,000 in minted gold and bullion. Reno and Virginia City seethed with excitement. Posses rode wildly into the Sierra and Washoe Hills and the gunmen were speedily apprehended by Wells Fargo's implacable detectives. But the pattern of robbing the steamcars was set, and from that time until well into the twentieth century it became a major preoccupation of gunmen and thugs, many of whose names entered into the folklore of the Old West as desperadoes of distinction.

SOUTHERN PACIFIC RR

LUCIUS BEEBE

SOUTHERN PACIFIC

Throughout the closing decades of steam, the ruling motive power of the Southern Pacific in the High Sierras of California and Nevada was the giant cab-first Mallets, shown on this page and specially out-shopped for the long snowsheds and abrupt curves of this rugged mountain territory. With the cab located ahead of the smoke exhaust and freed from the obstruction to vision which had characterized the long boilers of conventional locomotives, the crew was spared the inconvenience and danger of smoke and gasses in the tunnels while having a matchless view of the track ahead. In their lifetime the cab-first Mallets of the Espee with their tremendous trailing tenders were as indigenous to the Sierra as, before them, had been the diamond-stacked ten-wheelers which paused (BELOW) at Cape Horn while awe-struck passengers viewed the American River half a mile almost straight down.

[158]

Until the Westinghouse age, all brakes on freight and passenger cars alike were set by hand, and this was true of many early locomotives as well until a primitive form of steam jam brake was evolved to decelerate the more ponderous engines. Turning down the brakes on signal from the engineer's whistle up ahead could be at once perilous and a misery in winter as is suggested in this drawing by O. V. Schubert which appeared in *Harper's Weekly* in the 'eighties. The brakeman's lot was eased, but never exactly a sinecure, after Federal legislation caused the universal installation of the patent Westinghouse air brake. Fewer brakemen went under the trucks at Cisco and Colfax from the cartops of the Central Pacific going over The Hump. Operations in 1871 (BE-LOW) were simple, and in clement weather a brakeman could ride the cartops as his train rounded the mountain at Emigrant Gap and commune with nature.

Life aboard the Pullman Hotel cars of 1876 was an adventure for the touring players of the Jarrett-Palmer company in terms of red plush and inlaid woods, fine food and choice drink and snug nights in the patent uppers and lowers, which by this time were becoming an institution of travel and folklore at the same time. The chef in his galley, a miracle of convenience in microcosm, the restocking of the ice lockers with perishables at the brief stops as the cars whirled across the country, the clever porter who made down the berths at nightfall — all were objects of delight and interest to the passengers on the first transcontinentals. These drawings for *Frank Leslie's Illustrated Newspaper* were made by Walter Yaeger and Harry Ogden and represented stone lithography when reproduced in the finest flowering of that type of illustrative medium.

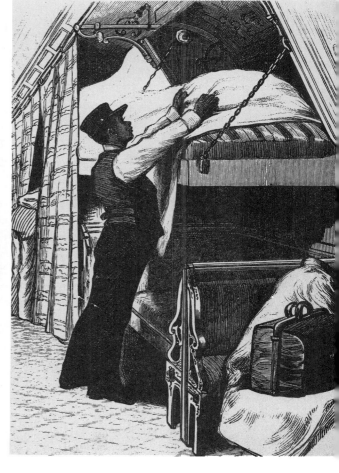

In 1876, the Centennial Year of American Independence, seven full days and nights, with changes of cars at Chicago and Omaha, were conventional time between New York and the Pacific Coast. When, therefore, a specially chartered train filled with theatrical celebrities and newspapermen made the passage from coast to coast in the record time of eighty-four hours, Americans followed the magnificently publicized event with awed enthusiasm not to be duplicated until the first transatlantic airplane flight of Colonel Charles A. Lindbergh half a century later. *The Lightning Express* was chartered by Henry Jarrett of Jarrett & Palmer, managers of the Booth Theater in New York, to transport the celebrated Lawrence Barrett and a distinguished supporting cast in time for opening night of "Henry V" at McCullough's California Theater in San Francisco. The project instantly caught the fancy of the public, and fantastic newspaper coverage was accorded the train's departure from Jersey City over the rails of the Pennsylvania and out of Chicago over the Chicago & North Western-Union Pacific-Central Pacific route to California. The actors rode in ornate splendor aboard the Pullman Palace Hotel Car, *Marlborough*, while a commissary car carried appropriate food and drink and the scenery rode in a conventional baggage car. All across the continent the train's passing was the occasion for the wildest excitement, and at Reno, nearing the end of its run, its approach was greeted with an exclamatory display of rockets and other *artifices de feu*. The run over the Central Pacific from Ogden to Oakland, a relay of 875 miles, including the High Sierra crossing, was accomplished by a single engine and a single engineer, Hank Small, at the driver's side. No. 149, a sleek 4-4-0, achieved immortality overnight. The sooty actors, weary but triumphant, were met at San Francisco by Warren Leland, manager of the eye-popping Palace Hotel and taken to a breakfast of grilled salmon, cucumber salad, filet of Beef Bernaise, cutlets of Minden lamb, escalloped veal, partridges sautéed in champagne, grilled Mallard duck, asparagus, strawberries and three kinds of eggs, shirred, with mushrooms, and rum omelettes. There were giants in those times. Framed above is No. 149, with Hank Small in his window, wearing a boiled shirt; taken at Reno in the noontide of their joint fame.

Now to th' ascent of that steep, savage Hill

"Paradise Lost"

In 1876, nothing gave such a vicarious sense of battle with the elements to a sketch artist, on the staff of *Leslie's* in his snug office in lower Manhattan, as drawing a scene in the wintry Sierra for his readers. This purported to portray four Central Pacific locomotives running a wedge plow through the drifts near Donner Summit. In the photograph below, more modern snow-fighting equipment is shown at almost precisely the same spot in the Sierra where a flanger hitched to the drawbar of a venerable Espee Consolidation waits to clear the switch points after a rotary has gone before it.

Despite their versatility and formidable tractive force, the Southern Pacific's Mallets had limits and this one, No. 4159, is only making the hill into Wendel, California, on the Alturas run on the second try. Once it had to back down two miles to the foot of the grade, leaving a brakeman behind to flag the crossing, then, belching smoke and sand, it came back again and made it on the second try for this dramatic action shot by Richard Steinheimer. Freight is mainly forest products from the Northwest and the Alturas line is an important short cut for the railroad. The drawing at the bottom of the page antedates the cab-first Mallets by some years and derives from the issue of *The National Police Gazette* of October 3, 1891. It was captioned "Took Duds and Money Too From a Fair Passenger Aboard a Central Pacific Overland Flier; Robbers Make a Rich Haul on the Pullmans Between Sacramento and Winnemucca, Nev." Like having to double on the hill, this, too, was a practice frowned on by the management with great frowning.

RICHARD STEINHEIMER

AUTHORS' COLLECTION

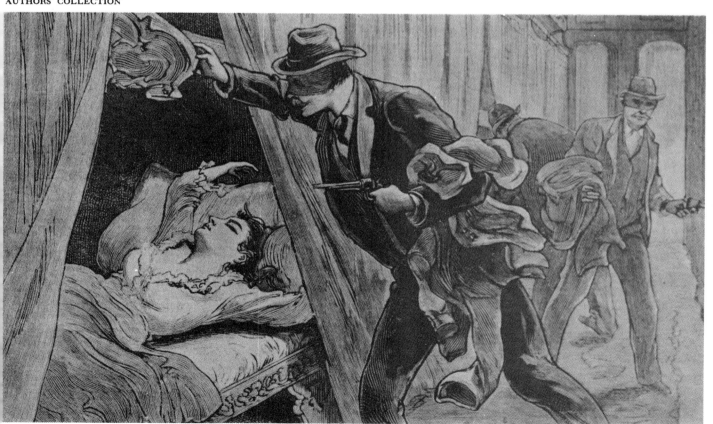

In the early years of Central Pacific operations across the High Sierra, all trains paused at Cape Horn so that passengers might marvel at the view, thousands of feet below, of the American River where the cry, "Gold, gold on the American River," first turned the eyes of the world toward California and unleashed a tide of emigration which to this day has flowed unabated toward the Pacific coast. The photograph here shown was taken in 1868 before the through connection was established at Promontory, and the time is reflected by the soldier's forage cap, worn by some recently discharged partisan in the War Between the States, come west to seek his fortune in the sluices and long toms of the Mother Lode.

Long a victim of train robbers in every guise and shading of desperation, the Southern Pacific encountered a new wrinkle in banditry in the 'eighties when thugs held up often-robbed No. 1 again near the Nevada-Utah line and gained access to Wells Fargo's strongbox by threatening to dynamite the baggage car in its entirety. So encouraging was the loot from such practices that in the banner year of 1895 there were no fewer than forty-three successful robberies of the Wells Fargo messengers aboard the cars in the Far West.

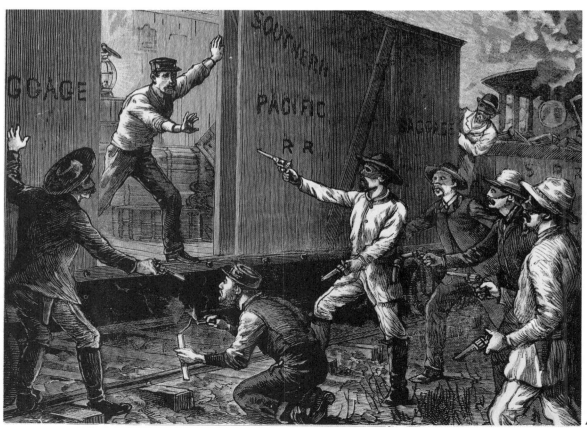

One regularly scheduled train about whose revenues the management of the road never complained was *The Fast Mail*, at Christmas sometimes running in two and three sections of seventeen cars each over the Southern Pacific's Overland connection. BE-LOW: *The Fast Mail* hits eighty a few miles east of Sparks as it crosses the Truckee River in 1946. ABOVE: the interior of a railway post office when mail trains were new.

LUCIUS BEEBE

NORTHWEST PASSAGE

HENRY R. GRIFFITHS, JR.   N.P. AT MULLAN, IDAH

For generations before the achievement, by the United States and Canada, of their eventual continental dimensions, explorers, cartographers and empire builders of many nations had believed in the existence of a water route or Northwest Passage from the Great Lakes to the already established shores of the Pacific. When the Northwest Passage became a reality, it was not a waterway but a complex of iron highroads over which, at the command of James Jerome Hill, Henry Villard and John Murray Forbes, the flanged wheel of American destiny rolled where the Long Hunters and the Mountain Men of the American Fur Company had gone before. From Chicago and St. Paul, ever north and west, spread the rails of primeval landfarings that were to become with the years the Northern Pacific, the Great Northern, the Milwaukee and Burlington roads. Short lines tapped the gold pockets of the Black Hills. Feeders reached for the limitless wheat fields of Montana. The Shay engines of lumber companies snaked out the ponderosa pines of Oregon from the misty Cascades. The Oregon Trail of Francis Parkman became the right of way of the Union Pacific. Where Lewis and Clark had camped along the Columbia, the smoke of the Spokane, Portland & Seattle's freight drags rose into The Big Sky. And where, in the imagination and dreams of that great navigator in the service of Francis I of France, Jacques Cartier, there ran The River of the West, *The Empire Builder* now flashed from the Great Lakes to Seattle in the space of two sleeps.

In 1940, steam still ruled the crack passenger runs of the Union Pacific in the North West. Here, in a camera portrait by Henry R. Griffiths, Jr., *The Portland Rose,* with eighteen cars bound from Oregon for Chicago, is getting under way out of Boise, Idaho. The locomotive is No. 823, one of the U P's giant 4-8-4s.

[167]

The annals of the Northern Pacific Railroad, which likes to call its right of way "the Main Street of the Northwest," have been those of some of the most exciting operations and spectacular steam railroading in the American record. Here under the big sky, amidst the towering peaks and running to the very littoral of the Pacific itself, steam ascended to heaven for nearly three quarters of a century to testify to man's going and coming in a spacious demesne of strongly pronounced character. On this page the camera of Henry R. Griffiths, Jr., has caught a Northern Pacific 2-8-8-2 compound getting under way up the winding and rugged grades of Lookout Pass near Mullan, Idaho. The tonnage limit for even so potent a locomotive is thirteen cars on this abrupt and curving grade. On the page opposite, the N P's *Alaskan* is shown leaving Missoula, Montana, westbound, for the climb over Evaro Hill with nine cars behind Pacific No. 2246 and Northern No. 2607. On this same platform in the year 1888, according to *The National Police Gazette* which closely followed such matters, unidentified ruffians forced Conductor Clark of *The North Coast Limited* to dance the cancan on the trackside. The road's scholarly president, Henry Villard, when informed of this outrage, is reported to have exclaimed, "Confound it! That's no way to run a railroad!"

HENRY R. GRIFFITHS, JR.

TWO PHOTOGRAPHS: HENRY R. GRIFFITHS, JR.

The four photographs on these two pages show the railroads of the Northwest with the elements in their most clement aspect and the thought of rotaries and flangers only an uneasy shadow on the division superintendent's mind. The Oregon & Northwestern is a short line for freight only between Hines and Seneca, Oregon, meeting the Union Pacific at Burns. Its traffic is largely in lumber and cattle, and here, of a fine summer's morning, its No. 1400 is heading fifteen cars up the hill from Trout Creek under a plume of black smoke to mark its going. At the left, the Northern Pacific's Compound 2-8-8-2, No. 4020, uses every pound of its tractive force to climb the west slope of Lookout Pass in the Bitterroot Mountains, near Mullan, Idaho, with a scant thirteen cars. On the page opposite, the Big Creek & Telocaset, running eleven miles from Telocaset to Pondosa, hauls five cars of merchandise behind Heisler No. 5. Like the Shay, the Heisler locomotive is gear-driven for often fantastic grades and, a *rara avis* at any time, has almost disappeared even in the Northwest of its greatest vogue. BELOW: The Mallet in Its Spoor. Northern Pacific No. 5113 waits in a siding for a meet along the margin of the Clark Fork in the Bitterroots, a massive portrait of N P power in the wild and desolate countryside that is its native setting.

HENRY R. GRIFFITHS, JR.

Smoke Plumes Against

The 149 mile long Camus Prairie Railroad in Northern Idaho is jointly operated by the Union Pacific and Northern Pacific Railroads for freight service only. On the page opposite, a U P 2-8-2 leaves Orofino with fifty-eight empties for the logging town of Headquarters, a pillar of cloud by day to mark the majesty of steam where the Long Hunters and the Mountain Men had gone before. Deep in the Blue Mountains of Oregon, following the course of the Powder River, there once ran the narrow-gage Sumpter Valley Railroad (shown on this page) connecting with the U P at Baker. Its traffic during its useful lifetime was in uncounted millions of feet of Oregon fir and its two Mallets, originally designed for the Uintah Railroad in Utah, were the only such locomotives ever built to narrow gage. Here against a background of Elkhorn Ridge is caught forever the wonderment and splendor of the little railroad in the bright noontide of its going. The Sumpter Valley is remembered with affection in the big woods as the Polygamy Central. It was built with Mormon capital.

The Big Sky

RAILROAD PHOTOS: W. J. PONTIN, TWO PHOTOS

Most aptly named of all American railroads, the Route of the Empire Builders, the Great Northern, bears to this day the stamp of its great original, James Jerome Hill, and its crack train on the run from the Great Lakes to Puget Sound, *The Empire Builder,* is named for him. No man and no railroad ever left more discernible traces of their going on the region they served and created than they did on the Great Northwest. On the page opposite, William J. Pontin has caught the engineer of *The Empire Builder* in the cab of one of the splendid 4-8-4 Northern type locomotives (BELOW) at Williston, North Dakota. Here, on the left, the fireboy gets the flimsies in duplicate, to confirm with those of the eagle-eye on the right-hand side, at Blackfoot Station, Montana. In the frame below, the veteran Fred Jukes stops a G N on the Vancouver-Seattle run near Blaine, Washington, back in 1924, when the northwest winter was still underfoot. Gigantic visions, prophetic men in patriarchal beards, vast distances and immaculate operations are all part of the pattern of a princely railroad.

AILROAD PHOTOS: W. J. PONTIN

FRED JUKES

HENRY R. GRIFFITHS, JR., TWO PHOTOGRAPHS

On these two pages appear a varied bag of action photographs depicting operations of four Northwestern carriers, two of them transcontinental main lines and two of them short-haul railroads. On the page opposite, on the Idaho Northern Branch of the Union Pacific two 2-8-0 helpers are cut into the middle of a freight consist on the grade near Banks, Idaho. BELOW: the well kept No. 9, a 2-6-2 of rare vintage of the Nezperce & Idaho, formerly on the roster of the Yreka Western, rolls slowly across a Trestle near Craigmont, Idaho. On this page (ABOVE) a Great Northern red-ball freight rounds a curve under a towering plume of exhaust at Wolf Creek, Montana, while below is No. 1400 of the Oregon & Northwestern as it pauses for breath at the summit of Trout Creek grade before doubling the hill with the second half of its train. The Oregon & Northwestern operates fifty-one miles of track between Hines and Seneca, Oregon, and connects with the Union Pacific at Burns. Lumber and cattle are, metaphorically, its bread and butter.

RAILROAD PHOTOGRAPHS: B. F. CUTLER

NRY R. GRIFFITHS, JR.

PAUL E. LARSON

Operating in the often sub-Arctic climate of the Great North Woods of Minnesota, North Dakota and Manitoba, the Minneapolis, St. Paul & Sault Ste. Marie Railroad Company, to give the Soo Line its full title, was once a carrier of character and individuality, given to exchanging buffets with the Storm King and fetching fantastic quantities of lumber and mineral wealth to less inclement latitudes. Its motive power was magnificently maintained and its schedules, like those of royalty, punctiliously observed. ABOVE: a mile or so north of Waukesha, Wisconsin, the Soo's single track crosses the old main line of the Milwaukee Road and an automatic interlocking system keeps trains of the two companies from tangling. On the page opposite, Train No. 50, with a proudly burnished 2-8-2 on the business end, rolls down the winter miles near Luck, Wisconsin in 1954. The Soo's passenger operations concentrate on the run between Chicago and Duluth-Superior, but in the tourist season it carries substantial numbers of pilgrims as far west as Portal, North Dakota, and Whitetail, Montana.

The Soo's operations in the vast logging regions of the North Woods date back to the almost prehistoric times when the lumber barons, newly emigrated from Maine and rolling in equally new wealth, started calling for plug hats, mistresses imported from Chicago and champagne to fill horse troughs, while the lumberjacks sang songs about Louis Sands and the patient oxen were motive power to roll the logs down the skid road to the waiting flatcars.

The Hines Lumber Company's No. 529 is an ex-Union Pacific 2-8-0, heading out of the tall timber east of Seneca, Oregon, one zero morning in the winter of 1955. The Southern Pacific's back door access to the Northwest is over its freight-only Modoc Division between Fernley, Nevada, and Alturas and Klamath Falls. Over it as many as four cab-first mallets sometimes hauled hundred-car trains. The one below is working at capacity on the head end at Wendel Hill.

HENRY R. GRIFFITHS, JR.

ROBERT H

It was forty-one degrees below zero at Marine, Minnesota, when the Soo's local pulled into the depot in 1954, and looks every minus degree of it. All cabooses are snug and cosy, but those of the Soo (BELOW) have to be supplied with outsize stoves and extra fuel bins to keep the crew from freezing in the winters of the sort grandfather used to remember, which are a commonplace in the regions the railroad serves.

FRANKLIN A. KING

The traffic of such ponderous locomotives as the Mallet No. 236 of the Duluth, Missabe & Iron Range, posed symmetrically on an overpass for the camera of Franklin A. King, is in iron ore for the seaports of Lake Superior and, eventually, the smelters and industrial manufactories available to Great Lakes freighters far to the south. The photograph below catches, on the private car siding of the Southern Pacific at Portland, Oregon, the profiles on adjacent tracks of Pullman observation cars devoted, respectively, to business and to pleasure. Nearer is the business car of the Espee's Superintendent of the Portland Division; beyond and identifiable by its red ceremonial carpet and jaunty yellow awning is the private car, *The Virginia City*, in Portland on the personal occasions of its owners in 1956.

　　LUCIUS BEEBE

Jointly owned and operated among the three terminals of its corporate title by the Great Northern and Northern Pacific Railroads, the Spokane, Portland & Seattle in the years of steam owned some of the most massive and effective locomotives of the Northwest. Here its Mallet No. 900, a 4-6-6-4 type, thunders up the one per cent grade at Marshall, Washington, ahead of 100 cars of manifest to make a resounding record of railroading under The Big Sky in the days of internal expansion.

Here one of the Milwaukee's ageless Prairie Type 2-6-2 switchers returns to Milwaukee after a day in the yards at Waukesha, Wisconsin, over a right of way that once was part of the original Milwaukee & Mississippi River Railroad. BELOW: in 1950 a Class N-3 Mallet 2-6-6-2, No. 58 crosses a trestle on the Metalline Falls branch line to form a silhouette of usefulness in motion in the autumn of its years and of the countryside around it.

PAUL E. LARSON

PHILIP R. HASTINGS

PHILIP R. HASTINGS

ins

Not all the transcontinental carriers serving the Great Northwest are Hill railroads or their affiliates: there are also the Union Pacific, Southern Pacific and the once-picturesque operations of the Chicago, Milwaukee, St. Paul and Pacific whose classic *Olympian* once ran in steam and electricity to challenge *The Empire Builder* and *North Coast Limited* on the passenger haul from the Great Lakes to Puget Sound. In the photo-study above, the drivers of the same Mallet No. 58 as shown on the page opposite are massively motionless for a meet at Newport, Washington, in the heart of the Milwaukee's mineral and lumber-haul region.

Sherman Hill

ROBERT HALE

To the pioneers who first encountered it—
the men of the Rocky Mountain Fur Company and the Astorians—the hill that was
later to be named for General William
Tecumseh Sherman was no more than a
landfall on the way to Independence Rock,
South Pass and the long trail to Oregon.
To the graders and tracklayers of General
Jack Casement, it was a challenge to the
Irish to be met with trainloads of rails, ties,
Ames shovels and forty-rod whisky. Two of
the ranking artists of their time who were
captured by the surge of railroading are
represented on this page. At the right,
Charles Graham, the celebrated staff artist
for *Harper's Weekly,* drew a night scene
when a Union Pacific train was delayed
near Green River by a herd of antelope.
BELOW: Dale Creek trestle, filled in in later
years, poses together with *The Overland
Express* for its portrait by the great Western
photographer, William Henry Jackson. The
road engine is a Brooks camelback, an
exotic design and almost unique in the
West, that enjoyed a brief vogue in the
U P 'eighties. On the page opposite, the
camelback's successor, one of the U P's Big
Boys, follows the Mountain Men westward
at Borie on the eastern slope of Sherman.

CHARLES GRAHAM

"WHERE THE DEER AND THE ANTELOPE PLAY"

NION PACIFIC RR

With the exception of the almost illimitable grass of its grazing lands, the biggest single factor in the existence of Wyoming is the Union Pacific Railroad. The biggest single factor in the Union Pacific's main line operations where its almost every freight and passenger consist must roll, be it from Oregon, San Francisco or Los Angeles, is a sculptured legacy of Pleistocene geology called Sherman Hill. The Hill, standing squarely in the line of survey between Cheyenne and Laramie, is a desolation in winter, a challenge to operating departments at all times and, until well into the sixth decade of the twentieth century, a perennial spectacle of steam and steel to fire the consciousness of every beholder. "I know of no place where man's going has left so little imprint on the earth," wrote Hamilton Basso, of Wyoming, but the U P right of way of fifty miles west of Cheyenne yard limit has been a tangible negation of this generality ever since 1867, when Jack Casement's track-laying gangs first arrived in Cheyenne to make that frontier village into what clergymen described as a sneak preview of Hell. General William Tecumseh Sherman himself, for whom The Hill was presently named, was more impressed with the engineering problem it presented than with the Indian menace of which some of his advisors spoke fearfully. "The whisky brought in by your graders and tracklayers will kill off every Indian within a hundred miles of your right of way," he told Casement, and so it was. As soon as it was established that the U P right of way had been located, not through Denver, but 100 miles to the north, the Queen City of the Plains promised to become a ghost town overnight and old Ben Holladay's stages into Cheyenne arrived with capacity passenger lists of prostitutes, madames, pimps, bartenders, faro-bank and monte dealers, tippers of the keno goose, music hall impresarios and assorted blacklegs, all the population of a progressive frontier community. All through the winter of '67, whose night life in Cheyenne is remembered with awe and admiration to this day, vast supplies of ties, switches, rail, trackplates and the necessary furniture of an operating division poured into the warehouses of the Casement brothers from Omaha and St. Louis. Ten thousand Irish tracklayers wintered in a sort of prolonged and glorious Saturnalia, but when the winds of April roared down Granite Canyon the tracks were halfway to Sherman Summit and by fall the end of track was in Laramie town. On wet, windy days, when the cloud level was at the top of the hills and the mist blew in constant rain squalls, the plains of Sherman were like the elemental sea. The drag freights beating up from Cheyenne to Dale Creek trailed smoke plumes like those of four stackers of the Atlantic in a time when ships burned coal, as God intended. Most of the aspects of Sherman Hill are elemental: its fantastic geology, its cloudy days and stormy nights, its tenacious resistance to human encroachment. It is appropriate that its conquest by man should have been through the elemental agency of steam. It is quite a hill.

RULING GRADE

The magnificent 800 Series 4-8-4 on the page opposite in a dramatic late-evening pose at Ogden, Utah, by Richard Steinheimer, is ready to move out with the first section eastbound of the now discontinued *Gold Coast*. It will take its train up Weber Canyon, across the Wyoming badlands and eventually up Sherman Hill. BELOW: the town of Sherman, on the Union Pacific's main line, as it appeared in the early 'seventies.

When it was erected, the Ames Monument, commemorating the memory of Oakes and Oliver Ames, the Boston tool manufacturers who supplied most of the equipment for the U P's construction, was hard by the right of way and trains paused to let passengers down at Sherman Summit to view this $80,000 red-granite tribute to Yankee sagacity. Relocation of the tracks in the Harriman administration, however, caused Train No. 1, *The Los Angeles Limited* (BELOW), to thunder through Buford, in later years nearly a mile away. On the page opposite, two sketch artists show Cheyenne depot in the years of the Black Hills Gold Rush. At the top, E. S. Hammack includes William Henry Jackson photographing a group of tourists on the platform, while (BELOW) Paul Frenzeny shows the bearded frontiersmen, Jewish pack peddler, monocled captain of cavalry, mining-stock salesman, con artist and Chinese laundryman, while the patient engine waits in the background, facing the still further, the ineffable West. No aspect of the awakening continent was possessed of greater fascination for the artist of the time than the railroad depots, which were becoming recognizable as the cathedrals of America to a far greater degree than any mere religious fane might be. Here was the center of life and motion, a pageant of animation depicted by a nation on the move to unseen destinies and distant landfarings.

LUCIUS BEE

RICHARD H. KIND

E. S. HAMMACK

PAUL FRENZENY

FOUR PHOTOS: LUCIUS BEEBE

The unceasing parade of steam power over Sherman Hill, in its great days, reached an all-time high during the Second World War when the smoke of twenty freights climbing out of Cheyenne at a single time was visible from the top of the grade, and the thunder of exhausts from the laboring Mallets rolling through Buford was a continuous symphony of power. In the above photograph the Union Pacific's No. 11, *The Idahoan*, streaks westward near Sherman station under a rolling cloud of smoke, while below the well-remembered *Forty-niner* takes water at Laramie in the years before the war. *The Forty-niner* was inaugurated to serve the uncommonly heavy passenger traffic to the San Francisco World's Fair. On the page opposite, both freight and passenger consists slow to pick up orders at Borie, eleven miles west of Cheyenne where the cutoff for Denver diverges from the heavily traveled main line.

[192]

ORDERS EAST AT BORIE; ORDERS WEST

1950

Between 1905—when the superb old-time action picture on the page opposite, showing a Union Pacific freight drag near Sherman Summit, was taken by Fred Jukes—and 1950—when Jim Ady caught the manifest being double-headed around the long curve at Sherman Station by a brace of long barreled 2-12-2s—the tonnage rating for Sherman Hill rose from twelve cars to seventy-odd and more when the Big Boys were handling it. But the elemental aspects of The Hill are changeless; the grade, the inclement weathers, the low visibility when the snow coats the signals and glazes the rails, the infrequent evidences of man's abiding in a hostile land. Below on this page, a pre-Big Boy Mallet at the head end of 100 cars essays the long, slow drag out of Laramie over the western approach of wintry Sherman.

FRED JUKES

1905

Over the Great Plains at sunset, its smoke trailing to far Wyoming horizons, a Union Pacific westbound freight drag drifts lazily down Sherman Hill on the page opposite toward Laramie while waiting for a clear board to the yards. Briefly, during the westward progress of Jack Casement's track gangs, Laramie had been Hell-on-Wheels and its flavor as an outpost of untranquil doings remained for years afterward. On this page, against the backdrop of a summer evening sky, two Big Boys start ninety cars of merchandise out of Cheyenne yards for an assault upon the Hill in pre-cutoff days. Long after steam had virtually vanished elsewhere in the land a glorious parade of the most beautiful and useful steam locomotives the world has ever seen continued in valiant tally over the U P main line all the way from Omaha to Ogden.

[197]

RETAINERS IN THE ROCKIES

Colorado railroading in the age of internal expansion exercised a particular hold upon the imagination because here, in perpetual strife against the elements and in conflict with the greatest barrier to transportation afforded by the continent in the Rocky Mountains, there flourished until the end of the era of steam, and in dramatic proximity, at once the most modern technique of railroading and the most antiquated. Until the beginning of the second half of the twentieth century, narrow-gage operations with stub switches still trans-shipped freight and passengers to main-line hauls powered by multiple Mallets and the most mature manifestations of the *expertise* of big-time railroading. The Denver & Rio Grande Railroad, pioneer in narrow-gage operations over scores of main lines and branches, still maintained rosters of locomotives and cars built to three-foot gage long after it had become a component in a complex of main-line carriers of continental dimensions. While the Mallets and Big Boys of the Union Pacific were rolling twenty-car Pullman trains on transcontinental runs to Denver over the Borie Cutoff, the three-foot Silverton branch of the Rio Grande was still carrying freight and passengers at the other end of the Columbine State in operations coeval with the Concord stagecoach and the Wells Fargo shotgun messenger. Elsewhere within the confines of the Shining Mountains little agricultural railroads such as the San Luis Central and San Luis Valley Southern flourished in magnificent profusion of eccentric properties and operations, baling-wire testimonials that the genius for individuality that had been the hallmark of the Long Hunters in the days of Bent's Fort on the Arkansas had not gone completely from the face of the earth. And there were industrial carriers such as the Colorado & South Eastern steaming among the ruined mineshafts of Delagua whose occasions were devoted to coal and iron and smelteries so obscure that their very existence was unsuspected in the communities they served. In Colorado the past was only yesterday for many years and the informed seeker was able to find the past in practical and functioning operation right to the end. On the page opposite, a Denver & Rio Grande Western freight, headed by a Class L-131 2-8-8-2 articulated Mallet, is moving a forty-eight-car train up the three per cent grade at Tennessee Pass at fifteen miles an hour. ABOVE: a two-car passenger run and the stylish locomotive of the vanished but much-loved Colorado Midland poses for its portrait by William H. Jackson at Divide. The year is 1885.

This narrow-gage action shot was taken in 1907 by Fred Jukes on Cumbres Hill and shows the changing times in the profiles of its engines. The helper engine No. 417 carried a diamond stack and the road engine, also a ten-wheeler, was equipped with the more up-to-the-minute straight stack then coming into vogue everywhere. Both were coal-burning locomotives, the diamond stack notwithstanding. Every Rio Grande engine of the period burned coal for fuel, it being, in Colorado, far cheaper and more easily available than wood. BELOW: in the Durango roundhouse, the narrow-gage ponies await increasingly infrequent calls to roll their tonnage over the grades to Chama, through the Pass at Cumbres toward the great world of standard operations at Alamosa.

The country ways of the Rio Grande's Silverton train, even in mid-twentieth century, established tangible continuity with an age of less urgent occasions and less hurried going. In the 'eighties, when the drawing at the right was made, the through varnish for Denver with David Moffatt and other millionaires aboard might not be available to such rustic satisfactions, but the Silverton-bound freight could pause beside the River of Lost Souls to refresh the water barrel in the caboose or even to let the crew snare a mountain trout for dinner. Occupied with the weighty concerns of a transcontinental main line, the Rio Grande never gave much thought to its humble and obscure Silverton train until tourists, campers and wild-flower pickers suddenly discovered its pastoral fascinations and bought passage in such numbers that, from a twice-or-three-times-a-week operation, it became necessary to schedule the run seven times a week during summer months. At the same time the films discovered the abrupt canyons and dramatic precipices of the Canyon of Animas and entire location companies put up at Durango to screen Westerns along the photogenic right of way above Rockwood. Victorian hotels in Silverton refurbished their mahogany bars and gas lamps shone once more where only lately the gloom of total oblivion had threatened.

UCIUS BEEBE

Between the year 1885, when William Henry Jackson posed this Rio Grande narrow-gage train on the cliff above the River of Lost Souls, and 1945, when Charles Clegg took the photograph, on the page opposite, of the twice weekly mixed train on the same run between Durango and Silverton, the proud and austere identity of mountain railroading in these remote parts had changed but little. In the noontide of its fortunes, in the 'eighties, Silverton had boasted through sleeping-car service to Denver and the narrow-gage private cars of Colorado's carbonate nabobs had rolled grandly through the high passes of the San Juans while their owners drank vintage champagne as chasers to their more accustomed bourbon and played poker for precariously stacked gold eagles. Six decades later, freight, fishermen and perceptive tourists still rode the narrow gage. The Rio de las Animas Perdidas, so named by Father Escalante who first explored the region, now and then rose and took the rails with it in winter, but always the narrow-gage iron reappeared, clinging tenaciously to the most spectacular three-foot run known to man. At the left, a Rio Grande Southern engine is dressed for a cinema role being shot in the identical setting of the other two photographs.

WESTERN COLLECTION

CHARLES CLEGG

ROBERT HALE

The town of Durango in the southwest corner of Colorado, although ensmalled by the abandonment of the Rio Grande Southern, is still narrow-gage capital of the world with three-foot tracks of the Denver & Rio Grande Western reaching north, east and south to Silverton, Alamosa and Farmington, New Mexico, respectively. From Durango to Silverton a narrow-gage passenger train still runs on regular schedule during the tourist months; on the other two divisions freight is the sole traffic. Above are the Durango yards at dawn, and elsewhere on these two pages views of the servicing of the narrow-gage iron ponies and of their moments of repose. Many of the railroad faithful, the true believers in steam, still turn their faces toward southwest Colorado as the pious Moslem turns his toward Holy Mecca.

These views of narrow-gage servicing in Durango, taken by Robert Hale, have about them implications of standard operations which have made three-foot railroading a microcosm of the fascinations of main-line carriers.

"Yea the smoke bites me, yea I drink the steam. . ."

SWINBURNE

Against a snow-mantled backdrop of the continental cordillera near Lizard Head, the Rio Grande Southern's No. 455, a 2-8-2, handles the smoky end of a sixteen-car extra, while No. 461 helps in the rear, in 1951, as the long annals of the Colorado narrow-gage carrier are drawing to a close. In the photograph below, the fireman of a Denver & Rio Grande Western engine takes sand at the Durango sandhouse against the grades en route to Alamosa, a study in narrow-gage power with implications of standard operations. On the page opposite, sunrise sees action at the Rio Grande narrow-gage roundhouse at Durango, while (BELOW) the Rio Grande Southern's No. 20 inches slowly along almost invisible rails in the meadows near Dolores.

[206]

Cloudy Trophies Against the Colorado Sky

FRED JUKES

If there is preserved anywhere a more magnificent action shot of turn-of-the-century railroading in Colorado than that on the page opposite, taken in 1908 by Fred Jukes on Cumbres Hill out of Chama, New Mexico, the authors of this book do not know of its existence. In it the diamond stackers No. 419 and 411 march splendidly up the grade with a second helper behind for a rendezvous with pictorial immortality. On this page the Rio Grande's narrow-gage No. 486 has its picture taken in Durango forty years later, while below, in another old-time scene by Fred Jukes, Nos. 417 and 207, both Baldwin-built, await orders at Chama in 1907.

CHARLES CLEGG

VARNISH FOR THE NABOBS

The Denver & Rio Grande Western's *San Juan* (PAGE OPPOSITE), when it closed its long and useful account on the Alamosa-Durango run in 1950, was the last narrow-gage luxury-name train operating in the United States. In the 'seventies, however, much glory and opulence had been the traffic of the three-foot cars in the Colorado Rockies. Aboard their diminutive private cars such grandees as Horace Tabor, Tom Walsh, John Morrisey, Dave Moffatt and tough old Charlie Boettcher played poker through the night watches for formidable sums as they rolled above the River of Lost Souls on the way to Silverton while empty champagne magnums illustrated their going for miles. Once archmillionaire Boettcher invited a professional gambler aboard his car, unaware of the fellow's identity and truculent ways, and a tense moment ensued when weapons were drawn. Usually the play was more decorous though no less spirited.

ROBERT RICHARDS

In the closing days of the narrow gage, most San Juan passengers rode the historic coaches (BELOW LEFT), but the de luxe way of life was still represented by two or three of the road's business cars dating from the old days and the parlor-buffet-lounge car *Alamosa* pictured at the lower right.

TWO PHOTOS: CHARLES CLEGG

On the morning of September 17, 1888, Otto Mears, "Pathfinder of the San Juan," ordered out the Silverton Northern Railroad's No. 100, the *Ouray*, hitched a boxcar and flat-topped combine behind and took a party of friends over the line to Red Mountain Station. Midway on the twenty-five-mile trip through the rugged Uncompahgre Mountains, a photographer, T. M. McKee set up his camera to take Mears himself, by the smokebox, and his guests, in the fearful and wonderful attire of the age, surveying his wilderness domain. Two other railroads, the Silverton & Red Mountain and the Silverton, Gladstone & Northern, were built by Mears into the mountain passes above Silverton itself. BELOW: a suggestion of main-line operations rides the double-header caught by Gordon S. Crowell as a narrow-gage red ball speeds west out of Alamosa where three rails accommodate both narrow and standard operations as far as Jara, fifteen miles out of town.

GORDON S. CROWELL

Casting a prophetic shadow across the Colorado hillside, the Colorado & Southern's narrow-gage 2-8-0, No. 65, carries white for an extra near Empire, in 1938, almost at the end of the narrow-gage run. BELOW: the R G S station at Ophir, hard by the famed Ophir Trestles, together with its main track and freight yard, is hollowed from the mountainside and its shelf held up by strong cribbing. The engineering involved in laying the iron of Otto Mears's improbable Rio Grande Southern across the high pass at Lizard Head, down the sensational trestles at Ophir, and over the precipitous grade from Placerville to Ouray, excited the admiration of a generation of railroaders who were cool to the triumphs of the Pacific Railroad.

The Rio Grande Southern, a railroad of much narrow-gage optimism among its sponsors but of constant deficits after its completion, was built in the 'eighties and early 'nineties to connect, via 162 miles of incredible operations, terminals a scant sixty air-line miles apart. Although revenue from carloadings at Rico, Telluride and elsewhere along its far-flung line were always insufficient, it survived for almost two thirds of a century because the territory it served was completely inaccessible to other transport. It lived on borrowed time through the Second World War, when rich deposits of materials necessary for the atom bomb were found along its right of way, and perished quietly a few years later. A double-header rolls out of Durango in 1945 (ABOVE), while most of its motive power was recruited from the D & R G W as shown below. On the page opposite, the R G S valiant No. 20 poses in costume for a film production in Durango yards, while below Richard Kindig catches D & R G W No. 454 on the two per cent grade near Cerro Summit. The Rio Grande Southern is with the ages but, together with the name of Otto Mears who built it, lives on as part of the legend of invincibility of Colorado's pioneers and the times over which they towered.

This rare old-time action photograph by Fred Jukes shows the dimensions of winter in classic times when it required three Rio Grande narrow-gage engines with a wedge plow at the head end to prevail against the deep drifts near Cumbres Pass on the Alamosa-Durango run. BELOW: a double-header starts out of Alamosa in 1956 against prophetic shadows of encircling gloom.

It must not be imagined, by a generation whose knowledge of narrow gage is largely secondhand, that the three-foot tracks and rolling stock which the Denver & Rio Grande brought to Colorado in the 'seventies and which, in a few years, spread to every gulch and proven diggings of the Rocky Mountain region, were either a frivolous or ineffectual aspect of railroading. On the contrary, the narrow gage was selected by General William Jackson Palmer and his hardheaded engineers as ideally suited to the limited finances at their disposal and later—when it appeared that the destinies of the railroad lay to the west of the great plains rather than in the Southwest of New Mexico and Old Mexico—it proved to be the only sort of railroad that could scale the incredible escarpments of the Rockies and penetrate the high passes leading to South and Middle Park. The three-foot gage trod out its appointed measure in the pageant of a westering nation with all the appointments and panoplies of standard operations in endearing microcosm. Narrow-gage sleepers followed the incredible right of way of the Denver, South Park & Pacific on overnight runs from Denver to Leadville and Jay Gould commented, "The Pullman Company gives us plenty of plush and polish for our money." Well-appointed narrow-gage diners ran over the original main line of the Rio Grande all the way to Salt Lake and private narrow-gage palace cars of the nabobs were spotted in the yards of far-off Silverton when all the world was young. The religion of narrow gage rode the three-foot tracks of a score of branches of the Rio Grande and of subsidiaries of the great main-line Union Pacific and Colorado & Southern. Only the Santa Fe, licking its wounds from its long encounter with General Palmer, was immune to the fascinations of narrow gage. In the year 1957, the last narrow-gage regularly scheduled passenger operation is over the superlatively scenic Durango-Silverton run (ABOVE) which, daily in summer and twice weekly in winter, skirts the high precipice at Rockwood above the abyss of Animas, the River of Lost Souls.

[217]

FRED JU

Six engines power a wedge plow on the Rio Grande narrow gage near Chama on the Alamosa-Durango run in 1907, from the collection of Fred Jukes. Any old-timer will tell you winters in those days were of epic and raging intensity, far worse than anything known to a later and degenerate generation.

In the coal-oil-lamp era of Colorado railroading, the camera of C. C. McClure caught the passenger train (PAGE OPPOSITE) of the Colorado Springs & Cripple Creek District Railway working steam up the two per cent grade with St. Peter's Dome in the distance. Known as "The Short Line" because it was ten miles shorter than the rival Midland Terminal and celebrated for its spectacular right of way into the towering Rockies, the C S & C C D was one of three carriers to serve the famed mines of Cripple Creek, which made millionaires by the score at the turn of the century. On this page, the *Silverton Train* on the narrow-gage Rio Grande run from Durango to Silverton edges gingerly through tall timber near Rockwood after a light fall of snow the night before. The time was February, 1946.

With the headwaters of the legendary Arkansas River visible in the meadows beyond its pilot the Rio Grande's Mallet No. 3615 rolls up Tennessee Pass in 1939 with fourteen cars of *The Scenic Limited* on the drawbar of a 4-8-4 road engine. BELOW *The Ute*, a red-ball manifest, thunders through Tunnel No. 8 at Scenic, Colorado, in the winter of 1938.

TWO PHOTOS: RICHARD KINDIG

OBERT HALE

Ruling grade on the western divisions of the Denver & Rio Grande Western on its Denver-Salt Lake main line, until it was relocated in 1913, was the four per cent haul between Detour and Soldier Summit, Utah. This photograph, showing five engines hiking a westbound passenger consist over the hill, is one of the classic action photographs of all railroading in the Far West and was taken in 1912 by Bill Shipler, a commercial photographer working out of Salt Lake, as had his predecessor in the long ago, Colonel Charles R. Savage, who was official photographer at the meeting of the rails at Promontory Point in 1869. At the left, one of the Union Pacific's equally classic Big Boys, diverted from the transcontinental main line to the Denver run, pants in the shadow of a coal tower in the Queen City yards before turning for the return haul to Cheyenne or possibly westward to Laramie over the Borie Cutoff.

Built by fabled David Moffatt, whom David Lavender has described as "a dull, patient, acquisitive man," with millions from the mines of Creede and Leadville, the Denver & Salt Lake Railroad started life as the Denver, Northwestern & Pacific and was designed to achieve the Mormon capital without a tip of the hat to either the Union Pacific or Rio Grande who were already there. Moffatt's money gave out when his line reached Craig, Colorado, but when it was eventually refinanced by a City of Denver bond issue they named the $18,000,000 tunnel it ran through after David Moffatt for having tried. Until it was absorbed by the Rio Grande, the D & S L was an autonomous entity with its own operations, rolling stock and motive power sharing traffic rights with the Rio Grande from Denver to Orestod, whence it went its own way to Steamboat Springs and Craig. ABOVE: an eastbound extra clears the East Portal of the Moffatt Tunnel behind No. 408, a 2-8-2, and a four-square Mallet 2-6-6-0 with forty-seven cars. BELOW: its daily passenger run behind a characteristic tenwheeler pounds up the two and a half per cent grade at Coal Creek.

GORDON S. CROWELL

ARLES CLEGG

A rare collector's item, in the realm of short-line operations, is the San Luis Valley Southern Railroad of Southwestern Colorado whose agricultural traffickings, like that of its neighbor the San Luis Central in potato harvests, occasioned the homespun photographs on this page. The S L V S connects with the Rio Grande's Alamosa branch at Blanca and extends thirty-five miles in the shadow of the Culebra Mountains to Jaroso near the New Mexican line. In the above picture, its solidly built Consolidation No. 106 is backing down to the road's one and only caboose, a veteran scavenged from its rich cousin, the Rio Grande, at Blanca. Below is the profile of the carrier's other engine, No. 104, identical to No. 106, waiting with steam up at the other end of the line with the road's single red wooden combine for the run back to Blanca. The country ways of the S L V S have always been characteristic of the individuality of Colorado short-line operations.

[223]

Pillar of Cloud by Day

RICHARD KINDIG

THE GLORY AND THE GLAMOUR THAT ARE GONE

Above is a court portrait of the classic American passenger train of the great tradition as the years of steam drew to a close: the Denver & Rio Grande Western's *Exposition Flyer* approaching Tunnel No. 1 out of Denver on its overnight run to Salt Lake where it will meet the Western Pacific. Coaches, and head-end revenue cars, diner, Standard Pullmans and brass-railed observation platform, here is the archetypal train that since the 'seventies had represented continental travel in America and cast the long shadow of its going across the American scene. In the drawing below, an artist from *Harper's Weekly* records the gloom of the evening Rockies in the early years of the Rio Grande's operations. On the page opposite, one of the Union Pacific's magnificent 800 Series, believed by many to be the handsomest steam engines of all time, pulls a local across the Great Plains at Sand Creek Junction, Colorado, in 1953.

LUCIUS BEEBE

The Midland Terminal, until it abandoned operations entirely in the early 'fifties, was only the vestigial trace of the once rich and powerful Colorado Midland, a main line from Colorado Springs to Grand Junction with continental ambitions. A hysterical Federal Railroad Commission ordered the Colorado Midland scrapped during the First World War and the Midland Terminal lingered on, serving the mines and smelters of declining Cripple Creek until the great Golden Circle smelting company built its own plant at the mine shafts and doomed the ore-hauling trade down the mountain. Here, in the last year of its operations, a venerable M T locomotive heads a consist of empty ore cars up the grade from Divide, assisted (BELOW) by a pusher behind its equally venerable, and perhaps even grimier, caboose.

SNOW ON THE COLORADO UPLANDS

A subsidiary of the Union Pacific, the Laramie, North Park & Western, reaches 111 miles south from Laramie, Wyoming, into the aptly named Snowy Range at Coalmont, Colorado, and is one of the handful of survivors of the once-numerous little independent operations which served as tributaries to the Overland Route of the U P. It takes from nine in the morning until five in the afternoon to reach Coalmont from Laramie in the line's caboose, longer when there are more cars than usual to set out at Millbrook, Centennial and Albany. The short line owns its own snowfighting equipment, including a massive rotary, and needs it a full five months of the year.

TWO PHOTOS: GORDON S. CROWELL

GORDON S. CROWELL

Collector's item, *rara avis* and purest gem serene of pastoral railroading, is the diminutive San Luis Central whose operations in the potato country of southern Colorado, over fifteen miles of light iron between Center and Monte Vista where it meets the Denver & Rio Grande Western, are so infrequent that local legend holds they are only accomplished in the dark of the moon. On the page opposite, the Central's only locomotive, No. 1 is shown in repose at the yards in Monte Vista and at speed with a load of high cars crossing the autumn countryside of Colorado in hard-to-come-by photographs by Gordon S. Crowell. On this page, at the left is No. 1's remarkable spark arrester, an arrangement of garden hose nozzles connecting via a length of gaspipe with the injector so that a fine spray controlled by the engineer will eliminate all fire risk in the dry season. This superb example of mechanical improvision is not known to have its parallel anywhere. Below and within sight of the Shining Mountains to the south, Union Pacific No. 1243, a ten-wheeler out of the legendary past sees action on the rails of the Saratoga & Encampment Valley, a U P subsidiary in mid-Wyoming.

JIM EHERNBERGER

SANTA
FE
TRAIL

The trail of the traders to Santa Fe led from the East and from the West toward the citadel of New Mexico, as well as from the seat of royal Spanish authority in Mexico City by way of Chihuahua. From Westport on the Missouri River, it led straight across Kansas, forking at Cimarron Crossing on the far side of Fort Dodge to follow the alternate route via Bent's Fort on the Arkansas or the *Jornada del Muerto* of the Cimarron Cutoff itself. To achieve New Mexico and the entire Southwest, it led up Raton Pass, the Pass of the Rat. From California the Golden, the wagon trains ascended out of San Bernardino through another similar pass, the Cajon. Through both of these east and west portals to New Mexico runs the high iron, the main line of the Atchison, Topeka & Santa Fe Railroad. In the Cajon trackage rights from San Bernardino to Barstow are shared with the Union Pacific, the one-time Los Angeles & Salt Lake Railroad. From the East and from the West the age of steam thundered on mighty landfarings over a route already established for centuries on the face of the continent: The Santa Fe Trail. On the page opposite, in dramatic panorama by Robert Hale, the Atchison, Topeka & Santa Fe's *Grand Canyon Limited* to a thunder of Ferdie Groffe music, sleek, steel and streamlined of Diesel, still requires the helper horsepower of one of the road's celebrated 3700 Series 4-8-4s as it breasts the grade of the Cajon near Summit. BELOW: sharing trackage rights from San Bernardino to the far side of Barstow, the Union Pacific advances and recedes in a pavane of power with the Santa Fe. In the action photograph by Henry R. Griffiths, Jr., two venerable U P 2-8-8-2s pound eastward behind a wartime consist of coal hoppers and assorted merchandise. The arrival in 1885 of the Santa Fe at Los Angeles precipitated a hilarious if costly rate war with the already entrenched Southern Pacific, which had just completed its own transcontinental line across Texas and was of no mind to tolerate a rival from Kansas. Passenger fares from the East were slashed as low as $10; trainloads of prospecting farmers pulled up stakes in Iowa and Ohio and land speculation in Southern California ran wildly out of hand. It was at this time that publicists for the two carriers inaugurated the orange-blossom-and-perpetual-sunshine promotion which has ever since been the stock in trade of the professional Californian.

AGE OPPOSITE: ROBERT HALE   HENRY R. GRIFFITHS, JR.

CHARLES CLEGG

Thunder In The Pass of the Rat

CLUB ROOM

Where now *The Grand Canyon Limited*, shown above after a light fall of snow, pounds up the Pass of the Rat under a towering canopy of exhaust, things once were different. Here Uncle Dick Wootton maintained a trading post and toll-road station with a bar of noble dimensions (BELOW), and here he plotted, while they drank improbable quantities of Taos Lightning, with the land-seer for the Santa Fe to secure the railroad's right to the pass before the arrival of the Rio Grande surveyors. As before and since, the grand design of empire was charted by strong men among the bottles and in dead of night.

Heading down the Cajon (ABOVE) a U P brakeman practices the time-honored calling of his name, clubbing down brakes on the high cars, while below a U P 2-10-2 helps a Diesel flying white over the grade.

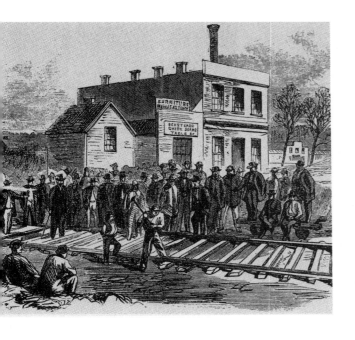

Did Colonel Cyrus K. Holliday on that blustery October morning in 1868, as he drove the first spike of the Atchison, Topeka & Santa Fe Railroad, at Washington Street between Fourth and Fifth in Topeka, really believe he would one day meet the then unthinkably distant Pacific? Topeka townsfolk smiled tolerantly at what they knew was the chimerical inclusion of the word "Santa Fe" in the road's corporate title. Yet, in the radiant photograph on the page opposite, the extra-fare limited, *The Chief*, roars out of Trinidad, Colorado, one gelid dawn during the Second World War on its approach to the Raton and the through run in forty-odd hours between Chicago and Los Angeles. BELOW: the eastbound *Chief* without a helper, climbs the west approach of the Raton near Glorieta, its smoke and steam exhausts twin banners of grandeur to mark its splendid going.

RICHARD KINDIG

SUNDAY AMUSEMENTS.

The Santa Fe's achievement of a gateway to the Southwest over the Raton Pass is inseparable from the legend of Richard Lacy (Uncle Dick) Wootton, shown below as he first arrived at Bent's Fort on the Arkansas before he was twenty. Already a Mountain Man of formidable celebrity, who had killed Indians beyond counting with Kit Carson, and operated a freighting route over the Santa Fe Trail, Uncle Dick, in 1858, opened the first saloon and gaming hall in Denver City and added to his already fabled reputation by the strength of the Taos Lightning he served. For his old age, he bought from Lucien Maxwell, also a noted Long Hunter, a toll road over the Raton into New Mexico, a monopoly of bonanza proportions since it was the only possible wagon route over otherwise impervious mountains. When the showdown came between the Santa Fe and Rio Grande, Uncle Dick threw in with Raymond Morley, advance land-seer for the Santa Fe who had ingratiated himself with the old gentleman by his phenomenal capacity for Taos Lightning. Eighty years after Uncle Dick and his burros had threaded the Raton, the Santa Fe's *Fast Mail*, headed up the grade from Trinidad, shook the sky with the exhausts of three engines, audible at the still-standing adobe where Uncle Dick and Mr. Morley drank deep in the night and planned to outfox the Rio Grande.

In the photograph below, by Herb Sullivan, a rail photographer who made his special hunting ground in the wild reaches of the Cajon, the *Los Angeles Limited* heads up the grade toward Victorville in an age when Diesel was unheard of and steam ruled the Union Pacific from Omaha to the Pacific. In the photograph above, Earl Webb, Union Pacific veteran, holds the air valve in service position as his engine drifts down the grade at twilight toward the yards of San Bernardino.

ROBERT HALE

HERB SULLIVAN

As a mountain snowstorm rages around his depot, the swing-shift operator at Summit in the Cajon hands up orders to the rear brakeman of a Union Pacific caboose as it flashes past in the night to form a dramatic vignette of railroading in the high passes and in the grand manner. BELOW, the first section of the *Los Angeles Limited*, running as a troop train in 1944, finds the Cajon in more clement aspect as it heads into the long tangent leading from San Bernardino to the foothills.

ROBERT HALE

Southwest Gateway

WILLIAM BARHAM

The station at the Summit of the Cajon is a study in infrared, with a Santa Fe smokebox carrying white flags to contribute to the composition, while (BE-LOW) *The Chief* pounds out of San Bernardino under a canopy of splendid soot to share trackage rights with the Los Angeles Division of the Union Pacific over one of the hottest stretches of rail in the entire Western continent.

ROBERT HALE

WILLIAM BARHAM

Service around the clock awaits the swift coursers of the Santa Fe insigne at division points along its far-flung operations between Chicago and the Pacific. ABOVE, while the *Super Chief* pauses briefly at San Bernardino before thundering into the Cajon, the engineer places green flags at his smokebox to show that there is a following section behind. The eccentric light streak shows the upward progress of his lantern while the photographer's shutter was open but before he fired his flash. BELOW: a service crew at La Junta, Colorado, greases the bearings and side motion of one of the Santa Fe's immense 4-8-4 greyhounds during its brief progress across the southeast corner of the Centennial State.

[241]

Fifty-six miles out of San Bernardino, ancient and farthest outpost of Mormon empire, the operator at Summit, at the top of the Cajon Pass, rules the grades from San Bernardino at the west end of the hill to Barstow at the east, surrounded by the special tools of his calling. He is Chared Walker, second-trick operator at this lonely post. BELOW: in the days when there was no *Super-Chief, The Chief* was monarch of the road as it thundered out of San Bernardino behind a helper and road engine, a pillar of cloud by day and a magnificence walking abroad in the land.

ROBERT H

LUCIUS BEEBE

At Fontana, just outside San Bernardino on the first leg of its 2,223 mile run to Chicago's Dearborn Depot, *The Chief*, extra-fare, all-Pullman de luxe limited streamliner for the upholstered names of the world, streaks for the East under a hot California noontide. The year is 1938, the locomotive one of the Santa Fe's giant 3700 Series which, with helpers at appropriate grades, will make the run all the way to Lake Michigan.

LUCIUS BEEBE

ACROSS THE GREAT PLAINS

Across the lonely immensity of the Great Plains along the Wyoming
Colorado border, the last of the Burlington's race of stately ten
wheelers closes the books on its long years of usefulness as it seek
the Cheyenne yards on its last run from Sterling, Colorado, a nobl
smoke plume against the summer sky its oriflamme of ultimate defianc
and at the same time its bid for pictorial immortality.

Of the three major railroads which set out across the Great Plains in the post-Civil War 'sixties—the Kansas Pacific, Santa Fe, and Union Pacific—the Union Pacific was immeasurably the best publicized. The Kansas Pacific, building out of Kansas City with the Cherry Creek diggings of Denver as its proposed objective, was shortly to be merged with the competition as part of the U P, but not before it had contributed notably both to American folklore and to the language. It was at Abilene that Wyatt Earp reportedly banished the town's bagnios and fandango houses to a district south of the Kansas Pacific right of way and evolved the phrase "the wrong side of the tracks." And it was at Abilene and Hays, among other roaring Kansas cowtowns, that railroad men established the first red-light houses as detailed elsewhere in this chapter. Having thus established itself in immortality, the Kansas Pacific quietly lost its identity, leaving the Great Plains to the U P and Santa Fe until the arrival of the Burlington, Rock Island, Missouri Pacific and other and lesser Johnny-Come-Lately carriers. The early days of Great Plains railroading were much of a piece both through Kansas and along the Great Overland & Pike's Peak route to the north: Indians, prairie fires, buffalo, blistering summers and gelid blizzards in winter, mighty tangents for the iron horse to stretch his legs and frontier towns where the fashionable tumult of fiddles, gunfire and breaking glass was never stilled. Railroaders then were a different breed of cats from what they were to become only a generation later. They enjoyed the girls of Juleburg and Dodge City impartially, and the Switch Key Saloon and the Box Car were named for the railroad trade which patronized them. They staged cornfield meets and ran their trains into the ditch and through open drawbridges with fine abandon until time and Rule G and engulfing respectability caught up with them. In the 'fifties, it is safe to speculate that the dispatcher did not have to send his callboy to Madame Minnie's place in Virgin Alley to recruit a head-end crew for the Union Pacific's Big Boy Mallets at the top of this page.

GREAT
PLAINS
PASTORAL

In the early days of Great Plains railroading after the tracks of the Kansas Pacific (BELOW) and Santa Fe had been laid across the long tangents of Kansas, the young and lusty train crews of the day added the phrase "red light" to the American lexicon. In the tough frontier cowtowns of Abilene, Dodge City, Hays, Wichita and Newton when a trainman with time on his hands between runs went on an errand of relaxation to a bagnio, it was conventional for him to hang his switchman's red lantern outside to facilitate the callboy on his rounds in the event the trainmaster wanted a train made up. The portion of the cowtowns devoted to love-stores was shortly known as the red-light district from the multiplicity of lanterns proclaiming the presence within of brakemen, conductors and members of the head-end crew. Railroaders of the generation were recruited from younger brackets of manhood, and respectability was yet to become merchandise aboard the common carriers of the period.

TWO PICTURES: KANSAS HISTORICAL SOCIETY

ROBERT HALE

Between Council Bluffs and Omaha, *The Overland Limited* in 1907 crossed the celebrated Union Pacific bridge across the Missouri under the massive bronze buffalo head on its top girder. The buffalo symbolized the gateway to the West and was suggested by Charles Francis Adams during his presidency of the U.P. AT LEFT: a few hundred miles to the west, Union Pacific's Mallet No. 4001 rests briefly from its labors in the yards at Rawlins, Wyoming. It is to be doubted if the head-end crews of either of these splendid machines have just been summoned from the festive couch their pioneer predecessors knew so well.

WYOMING STATE HISTORICAL DEPARTMENT

aily Morning Chronicle

PUBLISHED BY

HAS. DE YOUNG & CO.,

—AT—

. 504 Montgomery street, between Sacramento and Commercial.

SERVED BY CARRIERS AT

½ CENTS PER WEEK.

SINGLE COPIES, FIVE CENTS.

he Official List of Letters (furnished he Postmaster) is published in the CHRON- every Wednesday, in consequence of its e city circulation.

THE DAILY Morning

VOL. IX. SAN FRANCISCO, TUESDAY, M

OM YESTERDAY'S EVENING EDITION.

FROM THE JUNCTION.

XCURSION OF EX-GOVERNOR TANFORD AND PARTY TO TAYLOR'S MILLS ON THE WEBER RIVER.

TURN OF THE SALT LAKE PARTY—THEY REPORT THE ROAD IN A SOFT CONDITION.

quets and Festivities at Taylor's Mills—A Party of Visitors to Ogden.

ention of Union Pacific Trains in Weber Canyon in Consequence of a Broken Bridge.

al of Californians from the East—They mplain Bitterly Against the Union Pacific—More Californians Expected via White Pine.

BRIDGE AT DEVIL'S GATE STILL UNFINISHED—DELAYS AND INCONVENIENCES ARISING IN CONSEQUENCE.

[FROM OUR SPECIAL REPORTER.]

PROMONTORY POINT, May 8th, 10 P. M. (Received May 9th.)

Excursion to Taylor's Mills.

-day Governor Stanford, General Case-, the Superintendent of the Union Pa- and a large party went to Taylor's Mills.

Return of Salt Lake Party.

e party which left here for Salt Lake on day returned to-day. The roads are re- d to be in a soft condition, and the er was miserable during their excursion.

Banquet and Festivities.

eneral Casement to-day furnished trains to rnor Stanford and party, who made excursion from this point, being also lied with a bountiful collation and oceans ampagne. The healths of the officers of entral Pacific Railroad were pledged and al greetings extended to them by General ment, Superintendent of the Union Pacific. rintendent Campbell, of the Central, pro- d the health of General Casement and the rs of both roads, which was received immense applause.

Banquet at Taylor's Mills.

eral Hoxie, Assistant Superintendent of Union Pacific, entertained a large party to endid luncheon at Taylor's Mills, a hamlet e bank of Heber river. The most cordial ony and good feeling marked their enter- ment and all the toasts were drank with applause. A special train was placed at ervice of this party, and a visit was made gden, which lasted about twenty-four

Sketching the Scenery.

A. Hart, artist of the Central Pacific, y took numerous sketches of the scenery nd this point and vicinity, which promise ford complete views of this region.

Trains Delayed in Weber Canyon.

consequence of the breaking of a trestle e, the trains of the Union Pacific are de- d in Weber Canyon. It is expected, how- , that the bridge will be repaired to-day train will pass over to-morrow (Sun- . On this train are the officers of the n Pacific Company.

lifornians Returning from the East.

e train from the East arrived to-day. mong the passengers I note Major Jack man, Colonel Whiting, Judge Southard, onoma, Morris Speyer, agent of the Ham- and Bremen Insurance Company, J. Fran- and numerous other San Franciscans.

formed that if he attempted to play them false by sending for troops instead of money they would hang him to a tree. A guard was mounted around the car and scouts were sent out to give prompt information of the approach of troops or men. To-day the money arrived, the claims of the men were settled and they dispersed, allowing the train to proceed.

Closing of the Gap in the Union Pacific Road.

The gap in the Union Pacific road closed to-day, making a "Y" to turn cars on at this point. The Central Pacific will erect turn-tables on Tuesday.

[THIRD DISPATCH.]

LAYING THE LAST RAIL.

Ceremonies of the Occasion.

SPEECH OF DR. HARKNESS UPON PRESENTING THE GOLD SPIKE.

RESPONSES OF GOVERNOR STANFORD AND GENERAL DODGE.

A Friendly Contest for the Honor of Driving the Last Spike.

[FROM OUR SPECIAL REPORTER.]

END OF THE CENTRAL PACIFIC TRACK, May 10, 1869.

The last rail is being laid. A prayer is being offered by Rev. Mr. Todd, of Boston. The gold spike was presented by Dr. Harkness to Governor Stanford with the following remark: "Nevada offered the silver spike." Governor Safford, of Arizona, then presented a gold, silver and iron spikes, also making a speech.

Governor Stanford and General Dodge Respond.

Governor Stanford on behalf of the Central Pacific, and General Dodge on behalf of the Union Pacific, made appropriate responses.

Driving the Last Spike.

A telegraph wire is attached to the spike, and Governor Stanford has taken the silver hammer presented by the Pacific Union Express Company from Mr. Coe, and, assisted by Mr. Strobridge, will drive the spike for California and Nevada.

A Friendly Dispute About Driving Last Spikes—Screwing the Last Bolt.

A friendly contest has arisen for the honor of driving one of the last spikes. The honor of screwing the last bolt is accorded to J. W. Haines. The meeting has been called to order by Edgar Mills and in a few minutes the last rail will be laid.

THE LAST SPIKE DRIVEN.

Trains Make the Trip Across the Continent.

The following dispatch was received this morning. The time of the driving of the last spike was announced by the bell of the fire-alarm telegraph in this city, which was connected with the Western Union Telegraph line, and repeated the seven blows struck by Governor Stanford simultaneously:

PROMONTORY SUMMIT, May 10th, 12 M.

To the Press East and West: The last rail is laid—the last spike driven! The Pacific Railroad is completed to the point of junction, 1,086 miles west of the Missouri river, and 690 miles from Sacramento.

LELAND STANFORD,
Central Pacific Railroad.
T. C. DURANT,
SIDNEY DILLON,
JOHN DUFF,
Union Pacific Railroad.

TELEGRAPHIC.

[SPECIAL DISPATCHES TO THE CHRONICLE.]

From Gold Hill—Celebration Upon the Completion of the Overland Railroad—A Universal Firing—Sounding of Whistles, Leting off Blasts, etc.

VIRGINIA CITY, May 10th.—Gold Hill celebrated the connecting link of Eastern and Western civilization to-day by a shot from Fort Homestead, that set fifty-six mills and hoisting works' whistles blowing in unison, and a simultaneous raising of bunting. Thirty-eight guns were fired—one for each State in the Union, and five more, one for each of the Central Pacific Railroad Directors, and one double-shotted gun for Charley Crocker, the Superintendent. On the Virginia and Truckee Railroad line, all the blasts were let off at the signal and a continuous roar from Gold Hill to Empire City gave the welcome tidings that we were bound in fraternal bonds with our brethren in the East.

From Virginia—The Festivities Consequent Upon the Completion of the Railroad—Return of the Firemen—Attempted Suicide at Gold Hill—Etc.

VIRGINIA (Nevada), May 10th.—The completion of the Overland Railroad was duly celebrated by our people with all the noise at command that would make manifest the great joy they felt in the completion of the great national highway. The festivities of the day were concluded with a torchlight procession by the firemen, making a fine display.

Our firemen who went to Sacramento to participate in the celebration on Saturday returned last night and report having a good time generally.

A lady attempted to commit suicide at Gold Hill by cutting her arm with a razor. The cause was grief at the loss of a child.

The Kentuck and Crown Point mines remain closed. The Yellow Jacket is working all right.

From Los Angeles—A Mexican Girl Accidentally Poisons Herself—Small Pox Raving the Town.

LOS ANGELES, May 20th.—Last Saturday a Mexican girl bought a quarter of a pound of what was supposed to be salts at a grocery store, and, going home, swallowed the dose and died in five minutes. It was found that the dose was oxalic acid.

Small pox is creating considerable excitement in this city. We understand from good authority that there has been nearly twenty deaths, and that there are about forty cases now in town. The disease is confined mostly to the Mexican portion of the population.

The steamer *Orizaba* arrived at San Pedro at six A. M. to-day.

Supreme Court Order.

SACRAMENTO, May 10th.—In the Supreme Court to-day the following order was made: Martin vs. Levy—On motion of McRae & Rhodes, and filing stipulation, ordered that appellants have twenty days further time to file brief.

Telegraphic Connection Established With Fire Alarms in Eastern Cities.

SALT LAKE, May 10th.—We connect direct to-day with fire alarms in Chicago, Cincinnati, St. Louis, Pittsburg, Cleveland, Milwaukee and other Eastern cities. In addition to arrangements here and in San Francisco and Sacramento, at the last stroke of the hammer at Promontory Mountain the bells of the above cities will simultaneously ring out the news. A great celebration is taking place in Chicago.

G. H. MUMFORD.

Rejoicing at Stockton.

STOCKTON, May 10th.—At five minutes to twelve o'clock to-day, a small brass gun placed about fifty feet in rear of the Western Union Telegraph office in this city was fired by electricity simultaneously with the driving of the last spike on the Pacific Railroad.

EASTERN TELEGRAMS.

A GREAT FEAT.

The Gun That Announced the Completion of the Trans-Continental Road—How It Was Fired by Telegraph—The Process Described.

At precisely forty-six minutes past eleven o'clock yesterday morning one of the great guns at Fort Point thundered forth the announcement that the greatest materialistic achievement of this generation, and of the nineteenth century, was an accomplished fact. At the very second of time that the hammer in the hand of Leland Stanford gave the first blow to the last spike in the iron band that now spans the continent and unites the Atlantic with the Pacific, the loud reverberations of the cannon proclaimed the fact to our citizens, while in all the chief cities of the United States the great event was announced in the same manner—the fire bells being substituted for cannon in the Eastern States.

THE WAY THE THING WAS DONE.

The electricity for the local current was generated in a grove battery (sometimes called "nitric acid battery") of seven cups, furnished by the kindness of the Western Union Telegraph Company from their supply. The instruments used were a relay and key made by Lundbourg & Marwedel. The connection was made with the Company's line, No. 3, at Fort Point. It was effected with an insulator wire "of size sixteen," which was connected with a barbette gun on the eastern salient of the Fort. The gun was mounted on an ordinary iron carriage. It was loaded with a blank cartridge of about ten pounds of powder, the service charge for throwing a ball being from forty to seventy-five pounds. The vent was filled with fine powder, and a train made on the gun, in which was buried a copper wire with a platinum coil. As platinum can be heated to a red heat without melting, and is not easily fusible by electricity, a coil of this wire is preferred for purposes like the present. All the preliminary arrangements being completed, everything that was sent over the wire either way was read at the "relay" or temporary telegraph office established at the gun, and as the road approached completion the operator read every fresh item of intelligence, awaiting anxiously the preconcerted signal announcing that all was ready for driving the last spike.

THE CONSUMMATION.

At last the long looked for signal came. The enigmatical and cabalistic words and characters "S. S.," "Done! done!" were flashed over the wise, declaring the consummation of the mighty work. At the precise instant that the wire reported, the second "Done," the red-hot platinum ignited the train, and the thunders of the great gun awoke the slumbering reverberations of the heights and mountains from Telegraph Hill to South Beach, and from Tamalpais to Mount Diablo. At the same instant the electric spark produced simultaneous discharges of cannon, and peals of fire alarms, in Chicago, Cincinnati, St. Louis, Pittsburg, Cleveland, Milwaukee, and the other principal cities of the Union. The credit of making, the suggestion of the simultaneous discharge of cannon by electricity is due to Mr. David Hughes, while the successful and masterly manner in which the idea was carried out is to be attributed to the skill and science of Major A. W. Preston, who superintended and managed the practical details of the arrangements at Fort Point, acting under orders from General Ord, and the liberal co-operation of the Western Union Telegraph, actively represented by its local manager, W. Yountz, and lastly of the Committee on Fireworks of the late Celebration, who consummated the final arrangements and assumed the expense.

MILITARY NECESSITY.

The Fenians on the War-Path.

The Fenians who went over to Saucelito on their great annual picnic on Sunday last did not do themselves much credit by their conduct toward the citizens of that rural burg. The necessities of the Army of the Irish Republic caused them to drive American citizens off their own property. It is so unusual for a foreign military Power to exercise such authority that great indignation was aroused, and Fenianism got a pretty strong dose of good

It so fell out that on that windy afternoon of May 10, 1869, at Promontory Point, when destiny had a rendezvous with a track gang of Irish Paddies on the desolate Utah uplands, the photograph that was to become the most important single documentary picture in the history of the Old West and of American railroading was exposed upon his collodion plate, not by William Henry Jackson, dean of Western picture makers, but by Colonel Charles Savage of Salt Lake who was on the scene when Jackson was elsewhere. A few seconds before Colonel Savage's plate had been exposed to show the Union Pacific's No. 119 and the Central Pacific's *Jupiter* "touching head to head" as Bret Harte later had it, the strokes of the spike maul, wielded by dignitaries present, supported by aid from professionals when Vice President Theodore Durant of the U P was unable to strike it fairly, had been electrically connected with most cities of importance in the entire United States. The circuits were arranged to discharge cannon simultaneously in Chicago, Boston, Sacramento, New York, Pittsburgh, Cleveland, Milwaukee and San Francisco. Not since the news of Appomattox Court house had been flashed on the magnetic telegraph to the farthest corners of the Republic four years earlier had the American public been so moved. Everywhere fire bells tolled, anvils were smitten, prayers of thanksgiving were offered in holy places and glasses were raised and smashed in more profane resorts. Almost everywhere, as in the next day's editions of the San Francisco *Morning Chronicle* (PAGE OPPOSITE), editors devoted their front pages to the greatest material accomplishment since the completion of the Erie Canal. Unable to resist the appeal of tragedy amidst universal rejoicing, *The Chronicle's* correspondent in Virginia City on the Comstock Lode reported in his dispatch covering the scene of rejoicing in that Nevada community, that in Gold Hill, a suburb, "a lady attempted to commit suicide by cutting her arm with a razor. The cause was grief at the loss of a child." Promontory's emergence into the white light of notoriety lasted for several years after the Golden Spike until, by common consent of the carriers, the junction of the Central Pacific and Union Pacific was removed to Ogden sixty miles to the south. Promontory was celebrated for the rapacity of the colony of gamblers, blacklegs, prostitutes and deadfall proprietors who solicited the patronage of passengers descending to take the air for the sixty minutes usually consumed in servicing the engines and cars and trans-shipping the mail and head-end business. Madames promised complete satisfaction from their handmaidens with a minimum of delay and so adroit were the three-card monte throwers that, when they had cleaned a greeny of his money, it was the Promontory habit of chivalry to give back a five-dollar gold piece to see him fed the rest of his journey. With the building of the Lucin Cutoff across Great Salt Lake after the turn of the century, Promontory became only a place on the Utah map and was reclaimed altogether by the desert when the rails were torn up during the 1941 war.

San Francisco's celebration of the joining of the rails at Promontory began, characteristically enough, on May 9, a day before the ceremony itself in the Utah uplands, and lasted for three full days and nights during which time no place of business, from Market Street to the Seal Rocks, excepting only saloons and restaurants, was open. Here one of the several spontaneous parades of helmeted firemen, top-hatted citizens and enthusiastic urchins winds jubilantly through Montgomery Street in a haze of American flags and against a backdrop of the de Young brothers *Dramatic Chronicle*. On May 10, as shown below, the first regular transcontinental trains started from their terminals in California and at Omaha. For a few months they encountered wagon trains of settlers still heading west under the classic white tops, but shortly these disappeared, their going to close a mighty chapter in the American saga of continental landfaring.

The journey across the continent from Omaha to the Coast in 1870 required four days, but "every form of art paid tribute to the new miracle and gained popularity by so doing." Oscar Lewis is authority for the statement that "any play during the 'seventies that introduced a locomotive into its third act . . . was assured of success." The bearded bard of the Sierra, Joaquin Miller wrote: "There is more poetry in the rush of a single railroad train across the continent than in all the gory story of burning Troy." Miller availed himself of poet's license as the speed of the day was considered excessive if it topped twenty-two miles an hour, and fifteen was felt to be prudent. For years after Promontory, no illustrated periodical of the time appeared for a single issue without some reference, editorial or pictorial, to the Pacific Railroad. The line drawing above shows Ten Mile Canyon beside the Humboldt River in the middle of Nevada, a state by then in the wildest throes of the Comstock bonanzas. The practice of robbing the steamcars was meanwhile gaining in *expertise* in Missouri and Kansas, and train guards and baggage masters (BELOW) carried an arsenal in their head-end cars against possible molestation. Speeds might be slow on the Pacific Railway, but life was never for a minute dull.

To the first transcontinental passengers who rolled across the Union Pacific's right of way behind balloon-stacked teapot engines in the 'seventies, the prairies of Nebraska and Wyoming seemed endless. The average speed of first-class trains was twenty-two miles an hour, although in a few years much greater acceleration was possible due to relocation of the tracks and improvements in their grading and ballast. A sight that none who saw it ever tired to tell of was a prairie fire on the Wyoming plains from which the little trains of the age sometimes had to flee as depicted in the line drawing above. At the top of the page opposite, the Silver Palace Hotel Cars, shown in this rare old photograph from the files of the Southern Pacific, were placed in service between California and Promontory Point, Utah, where they met the Pullman sleepers of the Union Pacific, in 1869. They contained facilities for complete hotel service, served all meals, provided space for sleeping and relaxation and were the quintessence of luxury for the time and place. In the Gladstone valise and Macassar-hair-oil age nothing stamped a man as a seasoned traveler more than to have slept aboard a Palace Car. BELOW: a double-headed Union Pacific manifest rolls west out of Green River, Wyoming, where once passengers dined on antelope steak and washed in the morning aboard cars that boasted fresh water from hand pumps.

ENRY R. GRIFFITHS, JR.

Oriflamme of Speed

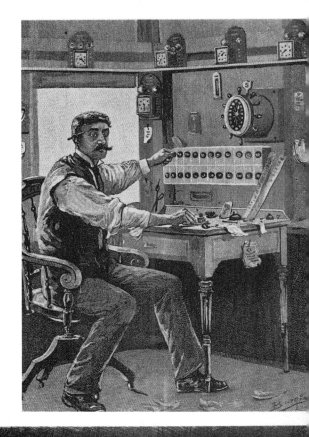

OTTO KUHLER: THE FAST MAIL

'RLINGTON RR

In the 'eighties of last century when government
contracts for the carriage of letters were highly
competitive and the railroads were making every
effort to establish new records for speed in their
delivery between distant points, the concept of fast
mail by train appealed to the universal sense of
drama. The nation thrilled to the vision of high-
wheeled locomotives, designed specially for speed
and endurance, manned by resolute nerves of the
same steel, racing through the darkened countryside
as mail clerks sorted the letters with consummate
skill in the wildly rocking cars. There was peril in
the fast mail, as was dramatically evidenced a few
years later in the wreck of the Southern's Old 97,
and the open drawbridge or cracked rail was ever
in the background. On the page opposite, Otto
Kuhler depicted *The Fast Mail* in one of the most
celebrated of railroad etchings, while in the panel
above a chief dispatcher of 1888 orders his division
over the company wire. At the top of this page a
Burlington fast mail train, *The Eli*, made such a
sensational action photograph for its time and place
as it raced through Sandwich, Illinois, at fifty-five
miles an hour in 1886 that the photographic Mr. Orr
had prints run up to sell. The idyllic side of a brakeman's life on the Burlington is suggested in the
drawing at the right. Much of the road's mileage lay
beside the Mississippi and riding the car tops in
summer could afford a matchless view of its ever-
changing vistas.

TWO PICTURES:
AUTHORS' COLLECTION

WILLIAM BARHAM

Under the administration of the great John Murray Forbes, the Chicago, Burlington & Quincy became one of the foremost colonizers of Western lands and, as shown on the page opposite, emigrants stayed warm and snug aboard the cars while train crews battled the monstrous snowstorms of the Great Plains in winter. Something of the pastoral charms of early operations was caught in the William Barham photograph (ABOVE) of an ancient veteran of the rails, a 2-6-0 outshopped in 1888, as it clattered down Burlington rails near Fort Madison, Iowa, in 1939. In the age of steam, migratory workers (BELOW) often rode the trucks without molestation from train crews because the railroads carried away the harvests they helped gather.

[257]

As the shining rails of the Union Pacific and Central Pacific reached ever toward their eventual meeting at Promontory Point in Utah, periodicals in the East and in Europe kept their readers fully posted on the progress of what had supplanted the now-obsolete Erie Canal in the public imagination as "The Work of the Age." The tracklaying gang shown here was sketched near Laramie in 1868 for *Harper's Weekly* by Theodore R. Davis, a celebrated Western artist of the time who had made his reputation as a Civil War correspondent and now, together with most of the rest of the nation, had turned his eyes to the West. Shooting buffalo from the cars, as shown below, became the classic shame and spoilage of an irresponsible people on the march.

FOUR DRAWINGS: AUTHORS' COLLECTION

In 1877, in an age when the newly opened West was the great American obsession, Frank Leslie, the Henry Luce of his day, whose *Frank Leslie's Illustrated Newspaper* was the *Life* magazine of a million readers, organized an elaborately staffed and widely publicized expedition to report the West to his readers. Inevitably many of the drawings of staff artists Harry Ogden and Walter R. Yaeger, which were sent back to the New York office of *Leslie's,* concerned life and operations of the wonderful steamcars which had taken on an new dimension of importance with the vast distances on the far side of the Mississippi. At one place in Nebraska a group of country newspaper editors boarded the Leslie train, set up shop and got out a souvenir edition while passing through Julesburg as shown in the above drawing. BELOW: one of the hazards of railroading in the Old West was the presence of organized bands of tramps who sought to ride the car tops and car trucks free and who often had to be dispossessed by force.

The boomer railroader who first rode the unballasted light iron across Kansas and Nebraska and followed the lurching engines into the Dakotas and the Arizona desert, was a different breed of cat from the unionized, domesticated and tamed hoggers and head shacks who came a generation or two later. In an age innocent of Rule G and teeming with frontier disorders, he carried a bottle of the dew of Bourbon county in one coverall pocket and a self-cocking bulldog revolver in the other, and the frontier was aware of him as it was aware of a surging population of cow pokes, bull whackers, stage drivers and timber cutters. Railroad Street in a hundred towns was lined with gorgeous saloons angled for the railroad trade: the Switch Key, Grabiron, Order Board, Roundhouse, Caboose, Main Line, Engineers Rest, Green Board, Signal Light and Pay Car. He headed west to the tune of fearful mating howls out of Kaycee, Omaha or Pig's Eye, secure in the knowledge that at every division point there would be a welcoming delegation of Dirty Girties, Minnie-the-Finns and Hog Foot Annies. Along the Southern Pacific's Arizona divisions local convention decreed that stolen switch lanterns should illuminate the doorways of red-light districts specially favored by the railroad trade. At Promontory Point, lately the scene of the meeting of the rails, enterprising madames promised satisfaction from their handmaidens to crew and passengers alike in the twenty minutes required for servicing the cars, and Promontory monte throwers and roulette dealers looked forward with the same anticipation as section hands to the advent of the pay car. In the lumber towns of the Great North Woods railroaders mingled on terms of mayhem with loggers who howled songs about Louie Sands and displayed fantastic capacities for Muskegon booze. From Manistee to Missoula and from Moberly to Fort Yuma, the boomer roved and ranged in an odessy of booze, battles and bagnio-doings that are part of the American epic. Domesticity and lodge meetings were still far down the tangent and around the curve. In the photograph below, taken at Tucumcari, New Mexico, where once a false-front night life roared happily and handy to the roundhouse, a brace of Rock Island 4-8-4s, hot from the head end of a westbound manifest, pant in the sun after turning over their consist to the Southern Pacific yardmaster.

RAIL PHOTOS: W. G. FANCHER

JIM EHERNBERGER

At the top of the page Union Pacific's train No. 353 *The North Platte Valley Express,* a daily run of mixed consist and homely occasions, pauses at Egbert, Wyoming. At the right an artist for *Leslie's* in the 'seventies depicts the mail being taken aboard a predecessor of the *North Platte Valley* at a similarly remote and lonely pause on a then even more remote and desolate Wyoming prairie.

FRED JUKES

FRED JUKES

Shortly after the turn of the century, when the photograph above and that below, on the page opposite, were made in Wyoming along the Union Pacific main line by Fred Jukes, action photography was a less assured technique than it was later to become. The U P's four-square No. 1913 snapped coming out of Rawlins at dusk, flanked by an old-fashioned wooden semaphore, achieved wide popularity in its time as a postcard entitled "A Night's Work Ahead." At the top of the page opposite, the U P's sunflower-stacked No. 711 was pictured at Sylvan Grove, Kansas, in 1900 and shows the resolute lines and stylish breeding which made the American Standard 4-4-0 archetypal engine so long as steam survived. BELOW: No. 1653 works a full head of steam on Sherman Hill in the grand manner of a noble tradition.

Attacks by hostile Indians on the steamcars crossing the Great Plains were somewhat more common in the sensational press in 1870 than in actual fact, but such forays were not unknown and this attempt to capture a Union Pacific train near Laramie, Wyoming, was drawn for *Frank Leslie's Illustrated Newspaper* in that year from the account of a passenger. Even the best mounted Sioux would have had trouble raising his Sharp's rifle to the window level of a U P locomotive of 1955 (BELOW) and probably would not have had the temerity to do so. The engineer could easily have discomfitted him by releasing live steam through his boiler exhaust under the cab.

Although the *San Francisco Overland,* which started running almost immediately after Promontory in the 1870s and which is coupled to the drawbar of the road-engine in this photograph of double-headed action, by Robert Hale, was always the last word in luxury of equipment, there was a time in its long saga of transcontinental landfaring when the platforms of its wooden coaches looked like those in the photograph below. Passing between the cars when the train was at speed in those times was a real hazard, discouraged for ladies and only tolerated in gentlemen by the management; grandfather going west on business buttoned the top button of his frock coat and clutched the brim of his silk hat firmly before venturing between the diner and his Pullman sleeper. When the forward car door was opened, a current of icy air or cloud of dust rushed into the car, and if the rear door was opened simultaneously, the through blast was a fearful thing. Many patents were issued for devices to prevent the opening of both doors at the same time, but the final and most practical solution was the double-doored vestibule which appeared in the 'eighties and, in the improved form of the entirely closed vestibule, has existed ever since.

[265]

Big Boy

Suite

Repose

At Rawlins

by

Robert Hale

"Come as of old, a queen untouched by Time . . . ."
Masefield

FOUR PHOTOS: JIM EHERNBERGER

For nearly half a century the Chicago, Burlington & Quincy's No. 919, a 4-6-0 of noble lineage and venerable mein, saw service on the Western prairies, coming at long last to the end of the line on the run between Campstool, Wyoming, and Cheyenne, with a three-times-weekly mixed consist of freight and an equally venerable passenger combine. Here, in the twilight of its years of usefulness, No. 919 aroused the affectionate interest of Jim Ehernberger who followed it upon its homely occasions until his files of negatives contained a full pictorial dossier of its way of life and country traffickings. Trailing clouds of remembered splendor as the sun goes down alike on its working day and the long tradition of reciprocating side motion on the Western uplands, No. 919 on these pages poses in the yards at Cheyenne and on its appointed rounds for a pictorial obituary of a way of life and a glory that is gone forever. A prudent management stored No. 919 at Sterling, Colorado, against the ever-present contingency of Diesel failure on its old accustomed run.

Ivan Dmitri

Rides

The Aristocrat

In 1932, the crack train of the Burlington's Chicago to Denver service,
The Aristocrat, operated over 1034
miles of mainline through the American heartland on a schedule of
twenty-six hours and thirty-five minutes with Pullman Standard equipment which was the last word in de
luxe rail transport of its time. Other
trains since that year have made it
on far faster schedules, notably the
Burlington's own *Denver Zephyr,*
but never in greater comfort or
more opulent surroundings. Its
matched Pullmans painted in pearl-
green with rose upholstery, rugs of
Oriental splendor, spacious private
and public apartments and superb
diner represented the apex of luxury
service embodied in the forty-fifth
year of operation of the flagship of
the Burlington fleet. Aboard its
sleepers and lounge cars *John M.
Forbes, Poudre Lake, Troutsdale*
and *New Manitou* the affluent and
powerful of the nation rolled in
cushioned ease across the Great
Plains to where the Rockies shim-
mered against the western horizon,
the Shining Mountains of the pioneers, the Long Hunters, the seekers
and finders of splendid fortunes.
Valet, barber and maid service,
shower baths, stocks of rare vin-
tages and a solarium observation
car made its progress that of a train
of imperial dimensions. Powered
by the Burlington's 3000 series of
4-6-4 locomotives, it was a thing of
smoky splendor in the lowlands of
Iowa and on the margin of the
Mississippi. On this page and on the
page opposite, Ivan Dmitri, the
celebrated industrial photographer,
fills an assignment to portray *The
Aristocrat* in casual images of its
head end and luxury interiors in
the great years of steam and golden
age of railroading.

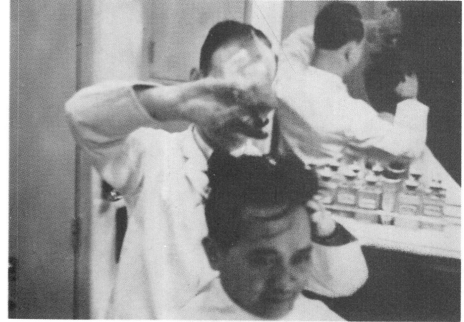

"LADIES IN WAITING"

OTTO KUHLER

Otto Kuhler's classic etching, "Ladies In Waiting," on the page opposite, had no prototype for his locomotives although traces of the Rock Island are discernible in their profiles, but the venerable ten-wheeler shown here in a night study by Jim Shaughnessy is unmistakably of the Chicago & North Western breed in the lordly manner of ancient times. No. 1405 was fired up at the historic town of Deadwood, South Dakota, one summer night when Diesel power failed on the division, a senatorial ancient recalled from retirement when upstart *arrivistes* faltered in the breach.

This noblest Roman of all ten-wheelers with its country spark-arrester and Union Pacific insigne was the last steam engine to see service on the U P subsidiary in the Wyoming prairies, the Saratoga & Encampment Valley Railroad. Upon its retirement a prudent railroad management stored the No. 1243 against the day when a serviceable steam locomotive should be an even greater wonder than it was in the year 1955.

Although not often associated in the popular imagination with such prairie carriers as the Burlington, Rock Island and Union Pacific as a plains-state railroad, the Chicago & North Western does in fact cover a vast territory of flat land in Iowa, Nebraska and Wyoming, its ranging iron reaching from horizon to horizon for hundreds of miles without perceptible grade or undulance. Here the North Western's Class E-2 Pacific No. 2905 has pulled off the Chicago-Minneapolis *Viking* for water at Madison, Wisconsin, for a classic pose in the servicing of steam. BELOW: a Union Pacific Big Boy is headed into the sunset both actually and metaphorically a few miles west of Laramie on the Green River run.

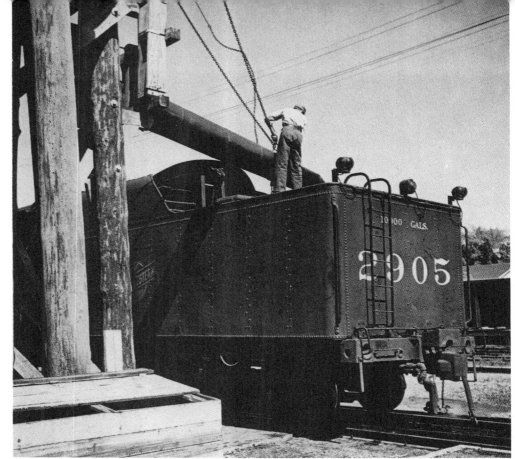

WILLIAM D. MIDDLETON

"THE TALL FAR-TRAFFICKING SHAPES"

PHILIP R. HASTINGS

The years move on toward the sunset, the tall, far-trafficking shapes,
Each with a bag of news to lay at a ghostly gate.

"JOHN BROWN'S BODY"

Turning their backs always to cities, the railroads of America sought out the country ways of the land, the level tangents across the prairies, the strait defiles in barrier ranges and continental cordillera, the narrow footholds along ageless waterways, wherever the iron might be bent to accommodate itself to the geology of its going and commerce promised at the end of the long landfaring. The land-seers sought out the way, the surveyors laid their chains and, lo, America was there, the new mechanic birth and the iron-handed age of the poet, the dreams of De Soto and Meriwether Lewis recapitulated in valve motion, drawbar pull and lighted Pullmans moving in the night. There was a poetry Americans could apprehend in the water tank at the edge of town, the shining rails laid under arching trees and across meadowlands to the heart's desire of home and country places. These were the roads and destinies Americans followed so long as there was something hid beyond the mountains of national consciousness. Happily the photographic camera was evolved in time to record something of this epic and its aspects of wonder. From the earliest days of railway travel when engines were fired from an open deck through the age of the cannonball-stove in the cars themselves down to the last final magnificence of counterbalanced side rods and six-wheel trailing trucks, the "instantaneous camera" as it came to be known, recorded the emergent genius of America for overland travel. On the page opposite, a tandem of Wabash Moguls, paced by meadow flowers at the tie's ends, face into the Illinois sunset. On this page, a New York Central 2-8-2, No. 1878, explores the coal-rich ravines of West Virginia at Rainelle over the tracks of the Nicholas, Fayette & Greenbrier Railroad which it operates jointly with the Chesapeake & Ohio.

PHILIP R. HASTINGS

Overland Limited

JIM SHAUGHNESSY

Heir to the most compellingly romantic name of the continental West, *The Overland Limited*, between Chicago and San Francisco over the connecting lines of the Chicago & North Western, Union Pacific and Southern Pacific Railroads, had its beginnings the day after the Gold Spike was driven at Promontory in 1869 and for more than three quarters of a century was an American travel institution of glittering dimensions. The original *Overland*, in the days of Pullman Palace cars of ornate design such as that shown on the page opposite, was so firmly established in Western folklore that its likeness, the right of way disputed by a California grizzly bear on the tracks, was the trade-mark of *The Overland Monthly* in Bret Harte's editorship. It was also the name of a famous cigar sold for many years by the impeccable firm of S. S. Pierce & Co., in far-off Boston, the image of the train gloriously emblazoned in red and gold on the box top. To have ridden *The Overland* at the turn of the century had all the implications of spacious ways and sophisticated travel a later generation was to associate with taking passage aboard the *Ile de France* or *Queen Mary*. English milords in monocles, European nobility in gaiters and ratcatcher suits, frock-coated Eastern bankers and the old nabobs of silver and gold of the West peopled its drawing rooms and rococo buffet cars. So august were the names that rode *The Overland* that New York Stock Exchange quotations were handed up en route and distributed by deferential conductors to Henry C. Frick and Simon Guggenheim in their staterooms. When the rare and radiant photograph reproduced below was taken just outside of Elko in 1916, *The Overland's* consist was regularly six cars powered by a high-wheeled Southern Pacific 4-6-2 as far as Ogden. In the last years of its identity before it was merged with the *City of St. Louis* on the San Francisco-Denver-Kansas City run, *The Overland* was powered through the Nebraska cornfields by the Union Pacific's 800 Class of splendid 4-8-4s whose prototypal example is shown on the page opposite. First and last, *The Overland* was a train of style and distinction, invested with a panache of aristocracy worthy of the Concord stages of the Central Overland, California & Pike's Peak Express Company that had gone before it down the Western years.

FRED JUKES

On Their Lawful and Useful Occasions

LUCIUS BEEBE

At Denison, Texas, where its beautifully shopped 2-8-2 No. 4153 is shown (ABOVE) just as it has crossed the Red River to work steam into town, the St. Louis-San Francisco exchanges valuable tonnage with a seldom-publicized complex of carriers known by three separate names as the Midland Valley, the Oklahoma-Adis-Atoka and the Kansas, Oklahoma & Gulf railroads. The MV is a bridge line to the four points of the compass, connecting Wichita, Muskogee, and Fort Smith with Baxter Springs, Denison, Tulsa and Oklahoma City, and doing business with the Santa Fe, Rock Island, Kansas City Southern, Missouri Pacific, Katy and Frisco. In early times (RIGHT) tramps were a major problem on the cars entering Denison and battles with train crews were a commonplace.

The Midland Valley's superpower, a 2-8-2 No. 601 equipped with the most mature resources of steam, lifts a noble façade at Denison in 1946, while (BELOW) an equally handsome Mikado with a tender tank rolls a short cut of high cars out of Carpenter's Bluff, Texas. The M V's equipment bears the titles of all three of its incorporated carriers on its nameboards and, in the days of steam, constituted an interesting study in the most modern practices on short hauls of great density and variety of freight.

TWO PHOTOS: LUCIUS BEEBE

WILLIAM BARHAM

Meet Me At St. Louis, Louis

LUCIUS BEEBE

Converging like dancers in a ballet pattern of continental dimensions, three varnish hauls of as many different railroads in the mid-'thirties head toward St. Louis from varied points of the compass. In Mr. Barham's picture, above, the Chicago & Eastern Illinois's Train No. 22, *The Zipper*, does seventy through Madison, Illinois, on the run from Chicago, while below the Alton's *Ann Rutledge* provides competition on the same haul. On the page opposite, the Missouri Pacific's *Kay See Flyer* from Kansas City runs through the morning mists to make its schedule at Maplewood, Missouri.

Focus and center upon which converge from every point in the compass the trains of twenty-one main-line railroads, gateway to the American Southwest, greatest railroad terminal in the world in number of carriers served, the St. Louis Union Station is more truly a cathedral reared to the American way of life than any other structure could conceivably be. The total mileage of the systems it serves is more than 100,000, and from its ramps and platforms it is possible to take direct or connecting passage to every one of the forty-eight states as Roman proconsuls set out upon the radius of Roman roads for Spain, Gaul and Britain, for Pontus and Bythinia and all the Empire of the East. The Union Station was opened in 1894, and ten years later it came into its own as a national institution, comparable to the White House and the Waldorf, when the World's Fair of 1904 gave the American people a new folksong: "Meet Me at St. Louis, Louis, Meet Me at the Fair."

WILLIAM BARHAM

Giant among Midwestern carriers whose operations range from Colorado to Texas, converging upon the St. Louis gateway to the Southwest, the Missouri Pacific Lines, embracing a variety of subsidiaries with such rich nomenclature as the Iberia, St. Mary & Eastern and the St. Louis, Brownsville & Mexico, is itself tied in bonds of corporate alliance with such continental carriers as the Western Pacific and International-Great Northern. Toward the close of its years of steam operations one of the Mopac's last strongholds of honored motive power was in the coal fields of Southern Illinois where its heavy 2-8-2 is shown stepping bravely out at Gorham with a coal drag in the Valley of the Little Muddy. Passenger service over the Missouri Pacific between St. Louis and Texas was for many years highlighted by the luxurious *Sunshine Special* whose club cars, characterized by mission décor with bars, observation lounges, soda fountains and cardrooms were one of the mature satisfactions of overland travel in the United States.

PHILIP R. HASTINGS

At the height of its effectiveness in steam, the Missouri Pacific had no fewer than fourteen different locomotive types in operation over its far-flung empire of steel ranging from ten-wheelers with clerestory cabs and gracefully archaic American Standard 4-4-0s to Russian decapods, 2-8-8-2 Mallets and Northerns of radiant magnificence. Shielded headlights, illuminated numberboards and faired-in air pumps mounted above the left-hand drivers gave Mopac power a distinguishing individuality. ABOVE, under a hot July sun, in 1936, one of the road's sleek, heavy Pacifics, No. 1159, thunders grandly through Webster Groves, Missouri, on the outskirts of St. Louis bound for Kansas City with a fast consist of mail and passengers. BELOW: a hostler backs 2-8-2 No. 1498 out of the roundhouse at Bush, Illinois, preparatory to heading a coal drag out of the Southern Illinois coal fields.

MOGUL SUITE

THREE PHOTOS: PHILIP R. HASTINGS

Inhibited by light bridge construction across the Illinois River at Meredosia against anything heavier in the way of motive power on its branch run from Bluffs, Illinois, to Keokuk, Iowa, the Wabash, as late as 1956, maintained a stable of veteran Moguls of great charm and character to animate its freight-only service over the seventy-five miles of country iron. On the page opposite No. 573 and No. 576 coupled tandem attack the grade to the west of Meredosia with thirty cars of merchandise on their joint drawbars. On this page is the massive cylinder and steam chest of No. 573 and below the double-shotted consist leaves the main line at Bluffs for its wayfaring among the cornfields and meadowlands of some of the most fertile farmland in the world.

The 2-6-0 wheel arrangement for locomotives originated in 1863 at the Rogers Locomotive Works for the New Jersey Railroad and was the first important variation on the American Standard 4-4-0 of universal usage. It was immediately known, because of the implications of tractive force in its generation, as "Mogul" and was widely used in freight service throughout the nineteenth century. With the coming of more sophisticated designs Moguls gradually disappeared from motive-power rosters, and the last to be outshopped were built by Baldwin in 1929 for the Blytheville, Leachville & Arkansas and eventually acquired by the Cotton Belt.

THREE PHOTOS: PHILIP R. HASTINGS

Almost nothing in the Wabash operation between Bluffs and Beardstown, Illinois, by way of Meredosia, discredits the illusion of railroading on the prairies at the turn of the century. The archaic Moguls, double-headed and rolling between the wild flowers that line the ballast out of Meredosia, are a page out of railroading in an earlier and less sophisticated time and place, a gentler age of hand-fired engines, coal smoke undulant against summer skies and rustic loungers in small-town depots down to watch the trains pass on their uncomplicated occasions.

In the above photograph, a member of the Wabash crew fills the sand dome of No. 573 in an operation almost as old as traction between wheel and rail, while below the valve motion of the ancestral Mogul, momentarily immobile at Bluffs, is a reciprocating ballade in classic meter of verse in four-foot, eight-and-one-half-inch dimension.

Times had quieted down for the Katy by the time, in 1946, the *Katy Flyer* (BELOW) was photographed rolling south out of Denison for Dallas, but things in the Texas 'seventies were livelier. In the contemporary magazine drawing, a freight brakeman is licking better than his weight in no-good Osages on the cartops, while the train captain peers apprehensively from a sort of primeval caboose in the background. Secretary of the Interior J. D. Cox on a tour of inspection of the Indian Territory had his silk hat punctured on a Katy observation platform by a pistol slug fired by a liquor-crazed halfbreed. Cherokees, Creeks, Choctaws, Kaws and Wichitas perished by the score under the car wheels where the brakemen tossed them as a matter of routine.

A specially heavy cross the Katy had to bear in the wide-open years of the Southwest was Poker Alice Ivers, second only to Minnie the Gambler and Madame Moustache in fame as a female operator of games of chance with vanadium-tempered nerves. Poker Alice liked the cars for skinning greenies. She found the Burlington almost ideally suited to her talents because of the bumpkin mentalities of the grangers who rode its country lines, but the Katy's early days were so populous with adventurers and easy money that she couldn't resist the trains to Texas. Poker Alice refused to carry firearms and startled the frontier by closing up shop on Sunday, but she had no compunctions about trimming the jaspers six days a week, which everyone felt was time enough. Here she is shown aboard one of the Katy's Pullmans running to the Red River as she turns the winning card on a victim in the stateroom from which she preferred to operate. She felt the smoking cars were unsuited to a woman of her fastidious habits in conning the suckers. Other pros, late of the now vanishing river packets on the Mississippi, were less particular. George Devol, a noted blackleg on the New Orleans-Natchez-St. Louis cold-deck circuit, offered the Katy management $10,000 a year for permission to play its cars without molestation and promised to cheat only clergymen, giving all others a fair break. The offer was declined but Devol rode the Katy trains anyway.

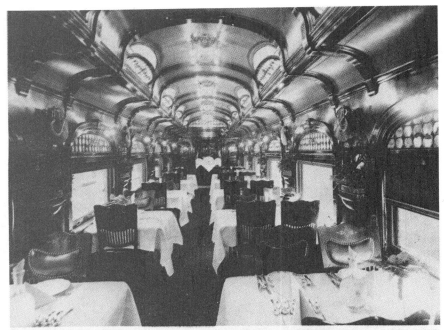

THE

CENTURY

Between George Boldt's Waldorf-Astoria Hotel at the corner of Fifth Avenue and Thirty-third Street and The Palmer House in Chicago where the bar was paved solid with silver dollars, there was, in 1905, only one thinkable and accepted agency of luxury transportation: *The Twentieth Century Limited,* crack express train and showcase of the New York Central & Hudson River Railroad and the world's best advertised flier. Aboard *The Century,* Chauncey M. Depew, Lillian Russell, Nellie Melba, J. Pierpont Morgan, August Belmont, Maurice Barrymore, Judge Elbert H. Gary and Charles M. Schwab bowed gravely or endearingly at each other as their station and occupation might dictate, over Louis Roederer champagne in the diner and retired to their drawing rooms to read their press notices in the New York *Tribune* or to smoke Prince de Galles cigars and plan mighty raids on the market, again as their sex and profession indicated. All of these exalted personages owned private cars of their own or could borrow them for the asking, but riding *The Century* was fully as satisfactory from the point of comfort and more so in prestige. There was, to be sure, the equally beautiful and equally fast, to the minute, *Pennsylvania Special,* later called *The Broadway Limited,* over the rails of the rival Pennsylvania, and Main Line Philadelphians like Alexander Cassatt and Drexel Biddle patronized the home railroad, but the world of *grande luxe* and high finance, the names that made news and meant millions, rode *The Century* and nothing else if they could help it. On this page are three interior views of *The Twentieth Century Limited* in the Delmonico Age which, together with maid and valet service and the dollar dinner that included both terrapin and filet mignon, served to make its appointments the talk and wonderment of the traveling world.

THREE PHOTOS: NEW YORK CENTRAL

In 1906, the time of *The Century* between Grand Central Depot and the La Salle Street Station was eighteen hours, and when the red carpet was rolled down on the platform for its departure, the same well-shod feet trod its pile as mounted the gangplank of the *Lusitania* to go to London or polished the brass rail in the men's bars at Sherry's or The Metropolitan Club in New York. The New York Central's literature advertised "Buffet, Smoking and Library Car, Observation Car, Stenographer, Telephone, Barber, Ladies' Maid, Valet, Fresh and Salt Water Baths, Manicure and Electric Lights Throughout." The telephone—shown at the right with a Central timetable of the period and a copy of *Harper's Weekly*, "The Journal of Civilization"—connected through "900, Thirty-eighth Street Exchange" at the New York end. *The Century* in the 'twenties and 'thirties, until the coming of streamlining, was powered by the stately race of Hudson Type 4-6-4 locomotives shown above, specially designed for the demanding miles between Harmon and Chicago.

THE OLD, OLD ENGINES

LUCIUS BEEBE

JOE REID THOMPSON

Deep in the misty bottoms of the East Texas timberlands the seven-mile Moscow, Camden & St. Augustine Railroad, connecting the company town of Camden with its Southern Pacific connection at Moscow embodies in its two daily train movements all the primal simplicities of operations in the prehistoric time when train orders, the telegraphic circuit and air brakes were not, and opposing trains approached each other on smoke orders implemented by hand-set brakes. Below, on the page opposite, its one graceful, tall-stacked Consolidation, built for the road in 1912 and in continuous operation ever since, rolls across a home-built trestle in the deep shades of the woodland it serves, while (ABOVE) its simplicity of valve motion pauses in the hot noontime at Moscow dreaming of many peaceful comings and goings over rails familiar from long acquaintance and ties even now rejoining the elemental earth from which they came. On this page, an ancient Mogul of the Wabash gets a dousing of valve oil before setting out on its daily run from Bluffs, Illinois.

A Mixed Bag in the Summer Midwest

In the early 'thirties, the Wabash Railroad rushed its merchandise under a cloudy overcast of soot over its main line between Chicago and St. Louis just south of Decatur, Illinois, behind No. 2919, PAGE OPPOSITE. At the left, the Akron, Canton & Youngstown's morning mixed train leaves Delphos, Ohio, behind a sightly 2-8-2 engine for Lima. Its single combine and mail car is at the far end of a mile of redball freight carded for the run to Bluffton, Arlington, Medina and Mogadore. BELOW: the Pennsylvania's *Jeffersonian* races into East St. Louis behind a streamlined K-4s at eighty-five miles an hour to keep its tight schedule on the New York-St. Louis run across a third of a continent.

CHARLES CLEGG

LUCIUS BEEBE

PRIVATE VARNISH

Throughout the age of steam and in common with ocean-going yachts, Fifth Avenue mansions, titled sons-in-law and English servants, the private railroad car was the hallmark of wealth and success, of established and enviable position in the American world of society and finance. The golden age of the private car was the bright noontide of the nabobs, who took pleasure in such costly and often beautiful conveyances and could afford their ownership; and from the mid-'seventies until the market crash of 1929 the private Pullman, ready to roll on its occasions of business or pleasure, was the ultimate panache of superiority in an acquisitive and ostentatious social order. The private railroad car was a way of life, and owners entered their cars in wildly competitive sweepstakes of elegances in the form of rare inlaid woodwork, gold-plated plumbing fixtures, sunken bathtubs, champagne cellars, crystal chandeliers, French chefs, English butlers and, in later years, air conditioning, deep freezes, functioning fireplaces and murals by celebrated artists. Successive generations of Goulds, Harrimans, Vanderbilts, Wideners, Fricks, Whitneys, Mellons and Huttons were known by their private cars as well as for their yachts, Florida estates and racing stables. Celebrated stars of opera and the stage—Edwin Booth, Lawrence Barrett, Adelina Patti, Paderewski, E. H. Sothern and Fritzi Scheff—rode in them to professional triumphs in the days of the theatrical road, and heads of state—from Abraham Lincoln, who only used his private car after he was dead, to President Eisenhower—have used them for conveyance to the far places of the land. In its long history, the Pullman Company estimated that it alone had turned out some 450 private and business cars for railroad officials at prices ranging from $50,000 in the 'seventies to $350,000 for Barbara Hutton's *Curley Hut*. W. Averell Harriman's *Avis*, built for him when he was chairman of the board of Union Pacific, cost a reported half million dollars. For six decades of the American record no property or possession carried with it the implications of wealth, prestige and achievement of the brass-railed observation platform of the private Pullman riding grandly at the end of the name trains of the nation.

In a time before a sharp demarcation was drawn between private cars and business cars, the old-time photograph at the left shows a group of Union Pacific executives grouped on a pioneer business car en route to the ceremonies at Promontory in 1869. Among the frock coats and brief cases are Sidney Dillon, chairman of the board of U P, Colonel Silas Seymour, chief of consulting engineers, and Samuel B. Reed, general superintendent of the entire epic project. The rifles and revolvers above the central corridor doorway were not for ornament as long as the plains Indians lasted.

The second private car *Loretto*, when it was built for Charles M. Schwab in 1915 after the first *Loretto* (ABOVE) had become old-fashioned, was a miracle of luxury and convenience as is suggested by the rows of push buttons to call servants to Mrs. Schwab's stateroom. In the photograph taken forty years later, Bruce Dodson, a Kansas City insurance tycoon, takes his ease with members of his family aboard *Helma II,* once John Raskob's *Skipaway*. Like Schwab, Dodson bought and named his private cars in sequence, *Helma I* having originally been built for A. C. Burridge, Boston banker and conservative moneybags of an earlier generation.

Holiday MAGAZINE

Once, in a time when railroading possessed style and breeding, the Chesapeake & Ohio, a carrier of honors and antiquity, had twenty different wheel arrangements on its motive-power roster. Only two of this multiplicity of tractive devices in steam are shown on these two pages: the road's compact and beautifully styled Kanawah 2-8-4s, elsewhere known as Berkshire type, and shown on this page in No. 2718 drowsing in the Kentucky night at Russell, and, on the page opposite, the road's 2-6-6-6, the world's heaviest reciprocating steam locomotive excepting only the Union Pacific's Big Boys. More than 8,000 horsepower strained the stay bolts in the 2-6-6-6 boiler, its Lima-built trailing truck alone carried 189,000 pounds on six wheels. Above, on the page opposite: No. 1614 climbs up the New River Valley out of Russell, Kentucky, with eastward coal tonnage on one of its last trips before retirement. BELOW: a similar Class H-8 runs into the gathering cumulus of a thunderstorm as it follows the state highway out of Alderson, West Virginia.

WILLIAM RITTASE

TWO PHOTOS: RAIL PHOTOS
GENE HUDDLESTON AND BEN F. CUTLER

The St. Louis Southwestern Railway Lines, generally abbreviated to The Cotton Belt Route, represents the connection of the Southern Pacific, of which it is a subsidiary, between the Deep Southwest and St. Louis, just as its juncture with the Rock Island at Tucumcari, New Mexico, represents the Espee's direct southern connection between California and Chicago. Passenger traffic over the Cotton Belt, whose rails reach as far east as Memphis, has always been negligible, but freight abundant and profitable is suggested by the magnificent 4-8-4 No. 812, at the right, wheeling a mile-long string of fast merchandise south out of Texarkana in 1946. In the same year, *The Lone Star*, the road's only daily through passenger haul from St. Louis to Texas with Pullmans from Memphis, makes up time west of Tyler, Texas, on its long tangent to the oil fields of Corsicana.

CHARLES CLEGG

LUCIUS BEEBE

A smoky Consolidation head-pins a short merchandise consist over the Cotton Belt's undulant Texas right of way, a few miles north of Dallas on the run from Addison. Until the end of steam, the Cotton Belt's motive power reflected the well-bred standards of design and maintenance of the parent Southern Pacific.

Car No. 1 of the Cotton Belt, reserved for the convenience of its chief operating executives, is *Fair Lane,* once the sumptuously appointed private car of Henry Ford, here shown being switched to the private-car siding at Little Rock. Occupied at various times by such ornately named Cotton Belt nabobs as Judge Berryman Henwood, the road's receiver, and President Daniel Upthegrove, its beautifully appointed private apartments, showers, rosewood wardrobes and dressing tables, all reflect the exalted status of its first owner.